Contents

6

The Neglected or Abused Child, 68

7

Intake Investigation and Court Reports, 78

8

Rights Versus Needs, 90

9

Detention and Probation, 104

10

Probation and Treatment, 113

11

Correctional Institutions and Parole, 125

12

The Future of Juvenile Court, 138

Index, 149

Juvenile
Justice
as a
System

Juvenile Justice as a System

LAW ENFORCEMENT TO REHABILITATION

ALAN R. COFFEY

Director of Staff Development
Juvenile Probation Department
County of Santa Clara, California

•

Instructor, DeAnza College,
Foothill College, University of
California at Santa Cruz,
San Jose State University

Other books authored or co-authored by
ALAN R. COFFEY

PRINCIPLES OF LAW ENFORCEMENT
POLICE-COMMUNITY RELATIONS
HUMAN RELATIONS: Law Enforcement
in a Changing Community
POLICE AND THE CRIMINAL LAW
CORRECTIONS: A Component of the
Criminal Justice System
ADMINISTRATION OF CRIMINAL JUSTICE:
A Management Systems Approach
AN INTRODUCTION TO THE CRIMINAL JUSTICE SYSTEM
AND PROCESS
CORRECTIONAL ADMINISTRATION
CRIMINAL JUSTICE AS A SYSTEM: Readings

PRENTICE-HALL, INC. · *Englewood Cliffs, N.J.*

Library of Congress Cataloging in Publication Data

COFFEY, ALAN.
   Juvenile justice as a system.

   Includes bibliographies.
   1. Juvenile delinquency.   2. Criminal justice,
Administration of.   3. Rehabilitation of juvenile
delinquents.   I. Title.
HV9069.C528   364.36   73-18095
ISBN 0-13-514372-1

This book is dedicated to the women in my life:
my mother, Margaret D. Coffey,
my wife, Bev,
my daughters, Alison, Annette, and Alana,
and my granddaughter, Jenny.

Prentice-Hall Series in Criminal Justice
James D. Stinchcomb, Editor

© 1974 by PRENTICE-HALL, INC., Englewood Cliffs, N.J.

Printed in the United States of America

10   9   8   7   6   5   4   3   2

Prentice-Hall International, Inc., *London*
Prentice-Hall of Australia, Pty. Ltd., *Sydney*
Prentice-Hall of Canada, Ltd., *Toronto*
Prentice-Hall of India Private Limited, *New Delhi*
Prentice-Hall of Japan, Inc., *Tokyo*

Preface

This book, as the title suggests, is an introduction to the American system of juvenile justice. With emphasis on the "system," the relationships among police, juvenile court, juvenile probation, correctional institutions, and juvenile parole provide the primary focus of this introduction.

While this book is intended to serve college and university students, it is also written with the hope that it will be of practical value to the various juvenile justice subsystems in their related goal—police to probation, probation to parole, institutions to court, and so on. From this frame of reference, this book will be of considerable interest to anyone concerned with delinquency and youth problems—civic leaders, school officials, community recreation organizers, social work agencies, and concerned citizens.

Many people gave me direct and indirect help in writing this text. In particular, many teaching colleagues will recognize their influence on the content of these pages. Additionally, I would like to express my appreciation to Chief Juvenile Probation Officer Dick Bothman, his assistant Mike Kuzirian, and their boss, Santa Clara County (California) Chief Executive Officer Howard Campen, for collectively administering a model of well-managed and systematic juvenile justice; to Santa Clara County District Attorney Lou Berna, for directing the most perceptive group of prosecutors ever to face the perplexities of the changing juvenile justice system; to many juvenile court judges, particularly those of Santa Clara County, for their thoughtful encouragement; and to the extraordinary Mrs. Kay Cuevas, who helpfully recognized an early similarity between this book and the training programs that I direct. Finally, my deepest continuing gratitude to my wonderful family, who always choose to mention the few family advantages of writing books as though the myriad disadvantages didn't even exist.

1

Juvenile Delinquency: Its Scope and Impact

Concern with juvenile delinquency is anything but new: "When troubled by the delinquency in their midst, members of *every* society have sought to account for that phenomenon. The threat posed by 'ungovernable youth' has provoked a multitude of reactions and led to a variety of explanations."[1] In order to approach the "phenomenon" on the basis suggested by the chapter title, a definition of juvenile delinquency is needed. Needed or not, there are virtually no adequate legal definitions of the term;[2] there are, however, many less formal and some very useful definitions of delinquency:[3]

> *Juvenile delinquency* is a blanket term which obscures rather than clarifies our understanding of human behavior. It describes a large variety of youths in trouble or on the verge of trouble. The delinquent may be anything from

[1] B. Rosenberg and H. Silverstein, *The Varieties of Delinquent Experience* (Waltham, Mass.: Blaisdell Publishing, 1969), p. 3.

[2] See, for example, *A Look at Juvenile Delinquency* (Washington, D.C.: United States Department of Health, Education and Welfare, Children's Bureau) Pamphlet #380, p. 1.

[3] E. Eldefonso, *Law Enforcement and the Youthful Offender: Juvenile Procedures* (New York: John Wiley & Sons, 1967), p. 7.

a normal, mischievous youngster to a youth who gets into trouble by accident. Or he may be a vicious, assaultive person who is proud of his anti-social behavior. As a blanket term, delinquency is like the concept of illness. A person may be ill and have polio or measles. The illness is different, the cause is different, and the treatment is different. The same is true of delinquency. Like illness, delinquency describes many problems that develop from varied causes and require different kinds of treatment.

This is useful because it illustrates the difficulty involved in formulating a black and white definition of delinquency. We can think about the concept, but a variety of problems seem to prevent us from knowing exactly who is a juvenile delinquent. For example, one state jurisdiction may consider a sixteen-year-old burglar a juvenile delinquent, whereas in other states he may be an "adult criminal." Still other state laws may permit sixteen-year-olds to be considered either "adult criminals" or "juvenile delinquents," depending on such criteria as previous record of delinquency.

A previous record may include violations of state school attendance requirements, even though most states consider truancy as no more serious than Halloween pranks. But Halloween pranks, in still other states, may be classified as "malicious mischief," regarded and reported in much the same way as assaults and burglaries—and recorded in such a way as to influence the determination of whether a minor is to be handled as an adult criminal or a juvenile delinquent.

The distinction between juvenile delinquency and adult crime is probably clear in only one area: *those juvenile offenses that would not be crime if committed by an adult;* that is, offenses such as truancy, running away from home, being beyond control of parents, or similar family matters.

In all other areas, *even though the same illegal acts are involved,* the distinctions between delinquency and adult crime are vague. And because a discussion of the scope and impact of delinquency requires as clear a definition as possible, it is necessary to discover a valid and consistent conceptual distinction between adult crime and juvenile delinquency.

Accountability vs. Responsibility

Perhaps the most effective approach to clarifying the distinction between adult crime and juvenile delinquency, then, is an initial philosophical distinction between *responsibility* and *accountability.* The distinction can be understood from the following example set in the context of three initial considerations:

1. Imagine a state in which the deliberate setting of a fire in a residence is a felony—an arson seen as a serious crime punishable by many years in a state prison.
2. Further imagine that the state laws correspond to the federal law granting the eighteen-year-old the right to vote; that is, the state law defines as an "adult" one who is at least eighteen years old.
3. Imagine that juveniles are defined as any person seventeen years or younger—meaning that in no case can a person under eighteen be an adult criminal.

Given these three variables, consider the following cases of felonious arson:

1. An eighteen-year-old is arrested, tried, and convicted for burning down a neighbor's house.
2. A seventeen-year-old is arrested, brought before the juvenile court, and declared a ward of that court for burning down a neighbor's house ("wardship" and other juvenile court procedures will be dealt with in later chapters).
3. An eight-year-old is arrested, brought before the juvenile court, and declared a ward of the court for burning down a neighbor's house.

RESPONSIBILITY: CONCERN FOR WHAT RATHER THAN WHY

Even though the specific *act* of burning down a residence is the same in all three cases, only one of the three persons arrested is a criminal—in only one case is there more concern with "what" happened than with "why" it happened. The eighteen-year-old is criminally responsible because he is an adult; the two minors cannot be held criminally responsible and are juvenile delinquents.

The eighteen-year-old is, by the legal definition of his particular state, an adult who is obliged to accept responsibility for his illegal acts. The eighteen-year-old is a criminal because he is responsible for his crimes; he cannot be a juvenile delinquent for two reasons: juveniles are *not* responsible for their illegal acts; he is not, by definition, a juvenile (see list of initial considerations).

Delinquents may not receive adult criminal punishment because, after all, they are minor children. However, delinquents are accountable for acts that would be crimes if committed by adults and, because they are juveniles, they are also held to account for many acts that would not be crimes if committed by an adult.

This distinction between *responsibility* for crime and *accountability* for delinquency, then, becomes a key to understanding the scope and impact of juvenile delinquency. Accountability, however, is not an absolute. It is determined on a sliding scale that must be understood as part of the distinction between responsibility and accountability.

ACCOUNTABILITY: CONCERN FOR WHY RATHER THAN WHAT

Returning to the arson example, both the seventeen-year-old and the eight-year-old are delinquent; as such, neither is criminally responsible. Both are, however, accountable for their illegal acts, *but to different degrees.* In both cases, more concern is placed on why the illegal act occurred than on what the illegal act is. This concern relates to the age and maturity of the two children—the "sliding scale of accountability."

On a common sense basis, the older delinquent is much more accountable than the younger. In this case, after all, the older delinquent is only one birthday away from being an adult—one birthday from being criminally responsible. The eight-year-old, too, may in fact demonstrate "inadequate parental supervision" more than delinquency. Implicit in the term *ungovernable behavior* is the lack of adequate parental control. As it relates to delinquency, adequate parental control implies sufficient control to prevent delinquency. Of course, this definition also implies that parents of the delinquent are inadequate. Were it possible to define a parent as inadequate simply because his child were delinquent, all parents would be inadequate to some degree.

Parental control must necessarily diminish during the child-rearing process. The totally dependent infant grows into a self-sufficient adult, and, as he does so, the parent's influence and control diminishes—at least in healthy families. It is then predictable, indeed desirable, that the parent not govern the teenager with the same rigidity as the toddler. Parental control alone, then, is inadequate to prevent delinquency. Yet parental control is the key variable in prevention, for it remains clear that the one thing *all* juvenile delinquents have in common (no matter how delinquency is defined) is the absence of enough parental influence to have prevented delinquency. And the juvenile court, faced with an alarming increase in referrals, has little choice but to explore methods of *increasing the effectiveness of parental control.*

Parent–Youth Conflict

In the context of predelinquency, there is no way to determine the spread or severity of parent–youth conflict in the modern family. And, of course, it cannot be inferred that the volume of juvenile court activity directly reflects the magnitude of this conflict. But at least to the degree that parental influence has failed to prevent delinquency, juvenile court activity does provide a limited index of *trends* in this area. And regardless of the extent to which parent–youth conflict has increased and parental influence has diminished, there is ample indication that reported juvenile law offenses are on the increase. By including the parental-control variable in the discussion of accountability for delinquency, the inevitability of the sliding scale becomes obvious. The eight-year-old arsonist is accountable only to the degree that he can be expected to comprehend the responsibilities that will be his upon reaching adult status. To whatever degree he is unable to comprehend such responsibilities, he can scarcely be held either accountable or responsible—both considerations being the obligation of his parents.

INDEPENDENCE AND DEPENDENCE

Another way of stating this is in terms of a child's *dependence* upon his parents. The years between infancy and adulthood are marked by gradual but steady replacement of independence for dependence, and at any given age a child presumably has more freedom than he did when he was younger. In this sense, once he reaches adult status, he has complete freedom from his parents and he is also criminally responsible for his illegal acts. The child is accountable for his illegal acts to the same degree that he is dependent upon his parents.

Scope of the Juvenile Delinquency Problem

Undertaking a discussion of the scope of delinquency requires consideration of the fact that many children may commit delinquent acts and never be apprehended.[4] "It seems clear that most adolescents at some time commit delinquent acts but are not officially defined as delinquents. . . . To be defined as an official delinquent is the result of social judgments, in most cases made by the police."[5] Put another way, a person is delinquent when "somebody in authority has defined him as one, often on the basis of the public case he has presented to officials rather than the kind of offense he has committed.[6] This is of course a way of restating the philosophy that delinquency focuses concern on why an offense was committed rather than on the offense itself.

[4] See, for example, T. Sellin, "The Significance of Records of Crime," *Law Quart. Review,* 47 (1951), 489–504; see also "Measurement of Crime in Geographic Areas," *Proc. Amer. Philo. Soc.,* 97 (1953), 163–67.

[5] R. Bell, *Social Deviance* (Homewood, Ill.: Dorsey Press, 1971), p. 309.

[6] I Piliavin and S. Briar, "Police Encounters with Juveniles," in E. Rubington and M.S. Weinberg (eds.), *Deviance: The International Perspective* (New York: Macmillan, 1968), p. 145.

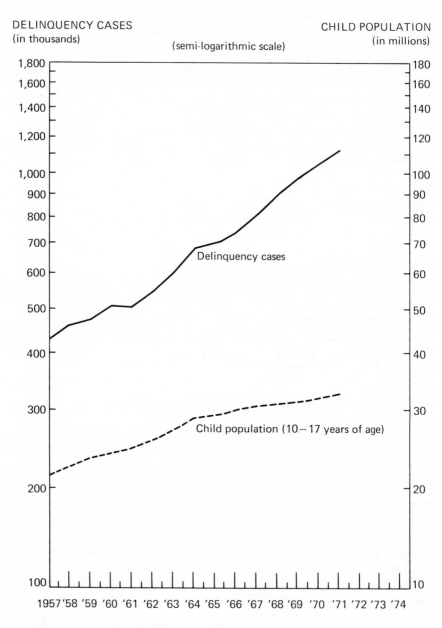

DELINQUENCY CASES
(in thousands)

(semi-logarithmic scale)

CHILD POPULATION
(in millions)

Juvenile Court Statistics 1971, U.S. Dept. of Health, Education and Welfare (Dec. 7, 1972)

Figure 1-1. Trend in Juvenile Court Delinquency Cases and Child Population 10–14 Years of Age, 1957–1971

Table 1

NUMBER AND RATE OF DELINQUENCY CASES DISPOSED OF BY
JUVENILE COURTS, UNITED STATES, 1957–1971[a]

Year	Delinquency Cases[b]	Child Population 10 through 17 Yrs. of Age (in thousands)	Rate[c]
1957	440,000	22,173	19.8
1958	470,000	23,443	20.0
1959	483,000	24,607	19.6
1960	510,000	25,368	20.1
1961	503,000	26,056	19.3
1962	555,000	26,989	20.6
1963	601,000	28,056	21.4
1964	686,000	29,244	23.5
1965	697,000	29,536	23.6
1966	745,000	30,124	24.7
1967	811,000	30,837	26.3
1968	900,000	31,566	28.5
1969	988,500	32,157	30.7
1970	1,052,000	32,614	32.3
1971	1,125,000	32,969	34.1

[a]*Juvenile Court Statistics 1971* (Washington, D.C.: Dept. of Health, Education and Welfare, Dec. 7, 1972).

[b]Data for 1957–1969 estimated from the national sample of juvenile courts. Data for 1970 and 1971 estimated from all courts reporting whose jurisdictions included more than three-fourths of the population of the U.S.

[c]Based on the number of delinquency cases per 1,000 U.S. child population, 10 through 17 years of age.

Having acknowledged that many children may commit delinquent acts for which they are not arrested, attention turns to statistics on those who are arrested. There is, however, increasing concern that these figures are less than adequate, if for no other reason than their reliance on reported offenses. Actual offenses can only be guessed at—the rape victims too embarrassed to report, the cars stolen by a "neighbor's kid," and so on.

This by no means minimizes the impact of reported offenses, which are the only reality to which the juvenile justice system can relate and which constitute a significant problem.[7] Prevention and detection may broaden the definition of reported offenses somewhat, and even the awareness that more offenses exist than are reported (or detected) is of value.[8] The

[7] See, for example, Figure 1-1 and Tables 1–4.

[8] See, for example, J. Eaton and K. Polk, *Measuring Delinquency* (Pittsburgh: University of Pittsburgh Press, 1961), pp. 3–7 and Chap. 9.

Table 2

NUMBER AND PERCENT DISTRIBUTION OF DELINQUENCY CASES DISPOSED OF BY JUVENILE COURTS, BY TYPE OF COURT, UNITED STATES, 1957–1971[a]

Year	Urban Number	Urban Percent	Semi-urban Number	Semi-urban Percent	Rural Number	Rural Percent
1957	280,000	63	113,000	26	47,000	11
1958	298,000	63	120,000	26	52,000	11
1959	295,000	61	127,000	26	61,000	13
1960	344,000	67	128,000	25	42,000	8
1961	350,000	69	119,000	24	34,000	7
1962	383,000	69	132,500	24	39,500	7
1963	414,000	69	146,000	24	41,000	7
1964	456,000	67	181,000	26	49,000	7
1965	470,000	68	183,000	26	43,000	6
1966	490,000	66	206,500	28	48,000	6
1967	525,000	65	235,300	29	50,700	6
1968	588,200	65	256,400	29	55,200	6
1969	646,600	66	280,800	28	61,100	6
1970	686,000	66	296,800	28	69,200	6
1971	717,000	64	331,000	29	77,000	7

[a]*Juvenile Court Statistics 1971* (Washington, D.C.: Dept. of Health, Education and Welfare, Dec. 7, 1972).

Table 3

NUMBER AND PERCENT DISTRIBUTION OF DELINQUENCY CASES DISPOSED OF BY JUVENILE COURTS, BY MANNER OF HANDLING, UNITED STATES, 1957–1971[a]

Year	Judicial Number	Judicial Percent	Nonjudicial Number	Nonjudicial Percent
1957	239,000	54	201,000	46
1958	237,000	50	233,000	50
1959	250,000	52	233,000	48
1960	258,000	50	256,000	50
1961	257,000	51	246,000	49
1962	285,000	51	270,000	49
1963	298,000	50	303,000	50
1964	333,000	49	353,000	51
1965	327,000	47	370,000	53
1966	357,000	48	387,000	52
1967	382,100	47	428,900	53
1968	425,400	47	474,400	53
1969	433,300	44	555,200	56
1970	472,000	45	580,000	55
1971	475,000	42	650,000	58

[a]*Juvenile Court Statistics 1971* (Washington, D.C.: Dept. of Health, Education and Welfare, Dec. 7, 1972).

Table 4
NUMBER AND PERCENT DISTRIBUTION OF DELINQUENCY CASES
DISPOSED OF BY JUVENILE COURTS, BY SEX,
UNITED STATES, 1957–1971[a]

| Year | Boys | | Girls | |
	Number	Percent	Number	Percent
1957	358,000	81	82,000	19
1958	383,000	81	87,000	19
1959	393,000	81	90,000	19
1960	415,000	81	99,000	19
1961	408,000	81	95,000	19
1962	450,000	81	104,500	19
1963	485,000	81	116,000	19
1964	555,000	81	131,000	19
1965	555,000	80	142,000	20
1966	593,000	80	152,000	20
1967	640,000	79	171,000	21
1968	708,000	79	191,000	21
1969	760,000	77	228,500	23
1970	799,500	76	252,500	24
1971	845,500	75	279,500	25

[a]*Juvenile Court Statistics 1971* (Washington, D.C.: Dept. of Health, Education and Welfare, Dec. 7, 1972).

reality of juvenile justice nonetheless remains reported offenses, and even sophisticated estimates of actual offenses are of little help in delinquency planning and programming.

When statistical reports from the Federal Bureau of Investigation and the Children's Bureau are compared with census figures, they indicate that delinquency has increased faster than the youth population in the last twenty years. But in terms of how common delinquency may be, the disproportionate increase in arrests may reflect little more than an increase in the practice of reporting these arrests to the FBI.

Compounding the difficulty is an "improved" classification system which is still in developmental stages.[9] The problem emerges when the classification system fails to match the statistical categories. For example, three of the statistical categories in the FBI's Uniform Crime Report (U. C.R.) are "city arrests," "rural arrests," and "suburban arrests." Attempting to apply these categories to any classification system that does not correspond to city, rural, or suburban arrests is confusing at best and,

[9] For one of the more innovative approaches, see T. Sellin and M. E. Wolfgang, *The Measurement of Delinquency* (New York: John Wiley & Sons, 1964), pp. 145–64; see also J. A. Mack, "Juvenile Delinquency Research: A Criticism," *Soc. Review*, N. S. 3:47–64 (1955), 56.

beyond confusion, offers nothing to clarify how common delinquency may be in any classification.

Representative state reports often simply categorize certain delinquent acts as "general offense," again confusing efforts to pinpoint and verify. And certainly the philosophical position that focuses concern on why a crime was committed contributes to the difficulty of knowing the scope of the problem. There is also the question of how many children commit but are not arrested for "delinquent tendencies"—a variety of offenses that would not be crime if committed by an adult. Do unreported "tendencies" exceed unreported delinquent acts?

THE PROBLEM'S TRUE SCOPE

The true scope of the juvenile delinquency problem, then, is exceedingly difficult to estimate. But the *reported* arrests of delinquents run to the hundreds of thousands every year. While less than 5 percent of American children appear before juvenile courts, of those who do appear, the majority have committed serious and repetitive offenses.[10] On the other hand, *self-report studies reveal that perhaps 90 percent of all young people have committed at least one act for which they could have been brought to juvenile court.*[11] But whether or not 90 percent of all children in fact commit delinquent acts, and whether or not the alarming number of children arrested every year is proportionately greater than those arrested fifty years ago,[12] delinquency is widespread. In its report on juvenile delinquency, the President's Commission on Law Enforcement emphasized the potential for social problems within the adolescent population:[13]

> On the whole it is a rebellious, oppositional society, dedicated to the proposition that the grownup world is a sham. At the same time it is a conforming society; being inexperienced, unsure of themselves, and, in fact, relatively powerless as individuals, adolescents to a far greater extent than their elders conform to common standards of dress and hair style and speech, and act jointly, in groups—or gangs.

[10] P. G. Garabedian and D. C. Gibbons, *Becoming Delinquent* (Chicago: Aldine-Atherton, Inc., 1970), p. 3.

[11] H. Sebald, *Adolescence: A Sociological Analysis* (New York; Appleton-Century-Crofts, 1968), p. 357.

[12] See, for example, the statistical studies of N. Teeters and D. Matza in R. Tunley (ed.), *Kids, Crime and Chaos* (New York: Harper & Row, Publishers, 1964), p. 51.

[13] The President's Commission on Law Enforcement and Administration of Justice, *Task Force Report: Juvenile Delinquency and Youth Crime* (Washington, D.C.: U.S. Government Printing Office, 1967), p. 10.

Adolescents everywhere, from every walk of life, are often dangerous to themselves and to others. It may be a short step from distrusting authority to taking the law into one's own hands, from self-absorption to contempt for the rights of others, from group loyalty to gang warfare, from getting "kicks" to rampaging through the streets, from coveting material goods to stealing them, from feelings of rebellion to acts of destruction. Every suburban parent knows of parties that have turned into near riots. Every doctor knows how many young unmarried girls become pregnant. Every insurance company executive knows how dangerously adolescent boys drive. Every high school principal is concerned about the use of marihuana or pep pills by his students. Every newspaper reader knows how often bands of young people of all kinds commit destructive and dangerous acts.

Impact of Delinquency

Judging the impact of delinquency without a precise estimate of its scope is difficult. Moreover, the difficulty is compounded by the inclusion of many noncriminal acts (family and school problems, for example), in the definition of delinquency (the distinction between criminal and non-criminal delinquency will receive further attention in later chapters[14]). In other words, one must assess the impact of criminal delinquency and the impact of delinquency that would not be crime if committed by adults.

IMPACT BY COST

One of the few tangible approaches to gauging the impact of delinquency is monetary cost, which is by no means the most significant aspect of the problem. The human stress, the family discord, the personal tragedies, and the emotional upheaval, not to mention the philosophical consider-ations, far outweigh monetary cost. But financial costs are far easier to measure than emotional and philosophical tolls.

Twelve years ago the estimated cost of operating criminal and juvenile courts and corrections . . . in one state . . . was more than $30 million a year. This amounted to $6.30 for each man, woman, and child who lived in the state. These figures did not include estimates of loss or damage resulting from the commission of offenses; the cost of law enforcement, arrest, or prosecution; capital investments in the maintenance of buildings, facilities, and equipment other than correctional institutions; and any extra-agency costs associated with

[14] A good example of the wide range of literature on this concern is W. H. Sheridan, "Juveniles Who Commit Noncriminal Acts: Why Treat in a Correctional System," *Federal Probation,* 31 (1967), 26–33.

trial, conviction, and imprisonment. The President's Commission on Law Enforcement and Administration of Justice estimated that national expenditures for police, prosecution and defense, the courts and corrections, exceeded $4 billion for the fiscal year ended June 30, 1965. These costs are borne primarily by the taxpayers at the state and local levels.[15]

Noting in particular the "$6.30 for each man, woman, and child" for services *other than* damage, police, arrest, prosecution, buildings, and facilities, the financial impact of crime in general (delinquency included) is extremely great—so great that the literature on criminal justice now includes some of the most advanced techniques in program management.[16]

IMPACT ON PHILOSOPHY

Less tangible but at least as significant is the impact of delinquency itself on the philosophy of how to deal with juvenile delinquents. For example, the impact of delinquency on police may differ from its impact on the juvenile court. The impact of delinquency on juvenile probation or those in charge of juvenile correctional institutions may differ from the impact on either police or juvenile court. One delinquent may be considered "wild," "insecure," or "disturbed," perhaps "in need of love" or even "a kick where it hurts"—he can elicit these reactions from people who share the philosophy that what he has done is not as significant as why he did it.[17] The philosophy does not determine the reaction to or, consequently, the impact of delinquency on those involved.

THE IMPACT OF SELF-IMAGE ON THE DELINQUENT

From birth, every human becomes increasingly aware of both *self* and *other*. Self-esteem develops only to the degree that the child learns to "make room" for *both* himself and other people. Implicit and explicit family rules help the child understand how much he can expect and what he should allow others to expect from him. He learns to accept or reject his own and others' feelings of anger, love, and sadness. Such family rules

[15] M. S. Richmond, "Measuring the Cost of Correctional Services," *Crime and Delinquency*, 18, 3 (1972), 243–44.

[16] See, for example, A. Coffey, *Administration of Criminal Justice: A Management Systems Approach* (Englewood Cliffs, N.J.: Prentice-Hall, Inc., 1974).

[17] A. V. Cicourel and J. L. Kitsuse, "The Social Organization of the High School and Deviant Adolescent Careers," in E. Rubington and M. S. Weinberg (eds.), *Deviance: The International Perspective* (New York: Macmillan, 1968), p. 132.

frequently determine the relation of self to other and influence later reactions to the rules imposed by society. Ultimately, there are only four possible means to make room for self and other:

1. *Count self in—Count other in.* When an individual has been raised in a family in which honest differences have appropriate rules for resolution, societal efforts to control behavior are generally acceptable.

2. *Count self in— Count other out.* Individuals in families who show considerable concern for "who is right" often find an absence of rules that would permit "agree-to-disagree" or other methods of "seeing-the-other-guy's-point." Rule structures in this family situation frequently generate hostility toward all rules in which "the other guy" might also be right.

3. *Count self out—Count other in.* Families operating from this frame of reference are the reverse of the preceding self/other position although they share relatively low self-esteem. In essence, family members focus great concern on "how-the-other-guy-feels" to the exclusion of how self feels. Although their lives may be generally unsatisfying, people from these family backgrounds customarily develop an extraordinary willingness to have their behavior regulated.

4. *Count self out—Count other out.* Family rules that, in effect, "disqualify" the importance of either the individual or the family group render the concept of rules useless. The rules that society seeks to enforce may or may not be perceived as relevant by the individual from such a family background, and other personality and sociological variables emerge as more significant.

THE UNKNOWN IMPACT

By far the most significant but generally unknown impact of delinquency is related to such personal considerations as family discord, tragedy, and emotional upheaval. While no overall measurement is possible in these areas, later chapters will explore one dimension of this impact that has to do with delinquency being, in some instances, the "training school" for adult criminal careers. At no time will I relate delinquency to adult crime in a "cause-and-effect" manner, but the delinquency history of many adult felons scarcely permits ignorance of the "human impact" of delinquency.

Summary

This chapter introduces delinquency as a concept and explores problems of definition: the contrasts between adult crime and juvenile delinquency, responsibility and accountability, and juvenile offenses that would not be crime if committed by an adult.

Delinquency is acknowledged to be widespread but, given the limitations of available data, it is impossible to know to precisely what extent. The impact of delinquency was considered in terms of monetary, philosophical, and human costs. The human impact is most significant but least possible to measure.

Questions

1. Relate the definition of delinquency at the beginning of the chapter to any of the subsequent problems cited with regard to defining delinquency.
2. Contrast adult criminal responsibility to juvenile delinquency accountability.
3. Discuss the sliding scale of accountability.
4. Relate concern with "why" rather than "what" to accountability; to adult criminal responsibility.
5. Explain the relationships of reported and unreported delinquency to the scope of delinquency.
6. Relate the number of children arrested to estimates of unarrested delinquents.
7. Assess the monetary impact of delinquency.
8. Discuss the various impacts of delinquency on police, courts, and probation.
9. How can the human impact of delinquency be most significant when it is impossible to measure?
10. Does delinquency have impacts beyond those discussed here? Explain your answer.
11. Do you agree that one should be more concerned with why a juvenile offense is committed than what it is? Why or why not? Should the same approach be taken regarding adult crime? Why or why not?
12. List some of the factors which, in your opinion, contribute to juvenile delinquency.

Annotated References

BELL, R., *Social Deviance*. Homewood, Ill.: Dorsey Press, 1971. An excellent survey of virtually all social problems.

ELDEFONSO, E., *Law Enforcement and the Youthful Offender*. New York: John Wiley & Sons, 1972. One of the more comprehensive works on the law enforcement procedures relevant to juvenile delinquency.

FLAMMANG, C. J., *Police Juvenile Enforcement.* Springfield, Ill.: Charles C Thomas, 1972. Excellent use of examples to clarify the relationships of child maturation, delinquent behavior, and criminal justice.

GARABEDIAN, P. G., and D. C. GIBBONS, *Becoming Delinquent.* Chicago: Aldine-Atherton, Inc., 1970.

KENNEY, J. P., and D. G. PURSUIT, *Police Work with Juveniles and the Administration of Juvenile Justice.* Springfield, Ill.: Charles C Thomas, 1972. Comprehensive coverage of the police role in juvenile justice.

ROSENBERG, H., and H. SILVERSTEIN, *The Varieties of Delinquent Experience.* Waltham, Mass.: Blaisdell Publishing, 1969. Explores an exceptional range of experiences influencing the delinquent child.

VEDDER, C. B., *Juvenile Offenders.* Springfield, Ill.: Charles C Thomas, 1971. A pragmatic approach to clarifying the concept of juvenile delinquency.

2

Theoretical Causes
of Delinquency

Before discussing the causes of delinquency, it is helpful to establish a philosophical context for human misconduct in general. Human behavior can be regarded as either within the control of each individual or *not* within the control of each individual. If the individual has complete control over his behavior, he is *self-determined.* If he has no control over his behavior, he is *determined*—that is, his behavior is determined by events, others, his past, and so on.

Theories of delinquency and crime, which tend to deal with influences, also tend to emphasize determinism. Nevertheless, during the discussion of these deterministic theories, it should not be forgotten that the very nature of juvenile and adult justice assumes at least some measure of self-determinism, or responsibility for one's conduct. Indeed, the establishment of an orderly society depends upon enough self-determinism to establish rules:

> Early societal rules that ultimately become criminal law might then be thought of philosophically as being society's formal effort to promote an orderly environment. ... With the goal of an orderly society, government,

particularly constitutional government, must take into consideration the relationship between society's power and the power of man's *will*. Much of what is called the Wisdom of the Ages probably deals with this very relationship in one way or in another. So also does this very relationship define most of what are called social problems. For in the final analysis, the individual power of the person is equally potent whether in support of or in dissent from the societal system of providing personal safety and property security.[1]

Clearly, a great deal of self-determinism is required if any society is to endure. And it also seems clear that, although we cannot completely isolate ourselves from things that "just happen," most of us feel that we have some control over our reactions to such events. At the same time, most of us feel that a few of our behavior patterns have been influenced, if not originated, by past situations. The theories that seek to explain the causes of delinquency are most useful if we keep in mind our own varied responses.

In much the same manner that an orderly environment is based upon a philosophical combination of self-determinism and determinism, most modern explanations of delinquency are a combination of theories. This is true for many reasons, not least of which is the critical attitude of many criminology scholars:

> At a time when "law and order" and "crime in the streets" have become major political issues, it has become increasingly urgent for criminologists and social scientists to put their own houses in order. The national concern with crime and violence has come at a time when criminological thought itself is in a period of crisis. The crisis may be briefly stated: traditional crime and delinquency theories have proceeded from the assumption that there are clear-cut distinctions between criminals and non-criminals. This false dichotomy has usually taken expression in the characterization of criminals as belonging to some criminal type. Whether earlier criminal type myths attempted to link the criminal to certain physical characteristics or mental deficiencies, the modern myth of the criminal type per se is in identifying the criminal with a particular social type—poor, lower-class slum dweller.[2]

But even though there is some validity to this criticism of theories, there nonetheless remains a great deal of value in understanding not only those theories to which this criticism refers but still other theories which may be individually in error but collectively of considerable value. And, as will be noted later in this chapter, the implications of each of the major theories offer something of value.

[1]A. Coffey, E. Eldefonso, and W. Hartinger, *Human Relations: Law Enforcement in a Changing Community* (Englewood Cliffs, N.J.: Prentice-Hall, Inc., 1971), pp. 53–54.

[2]Tony G. Poveda, "The Image of the Criminal: A Critique of Crime and Delinquency Theories," *Issues In Criminology*, Vol. 5, No. 1, 1970, 59.

Psychological Theories

The frequency with which discussions of the causes of delinquency include "psychological factors" suggests a wide range of theories in this category. Discussion of psychological causes, therefore, will be based on a variety of literature, all of which is relevant and cogent.

Sociological theories, presented later in this chapter, very often deal with the influence of the family. But recent interest in psychodynamics has brought the family into the theoretical framework relating delinquency to psychological causes. Psychodynamics is the system of emotional interactions which occurs in the family and other groups. These interactions usually develop into and can be observed as patterns of behavior. The concept of honesty can be used to illustrate how family psychodynamics may influence behavior.

FAMILY PSYCHODYNAMICS

So much a part of our culture is the faith and the honesty of very small children (at least to the degree that they can distinguish between fantasy and reality) that it is rarely questioned. It is just as common to assume that the older child is likely to be dishonest. The source of this disparity in honesty between younger and older children is not always clear, however. On a common-sense basis, it is clear that a small child's instinctive honesty is jeopardized by punishment for honest responses to such parental questions as "Who left this kiddie-car in the driveway?" Multiplying this subtle training a millionfold during a child's preteen years, it is scarcely surprising if the child's honesty does not become "flexible"— particularly if both parents and perhaps other family members "reward" honesty in this manner.

But honesty is only one of many dynamics that may be shaped by such training. And such unfortunate patterns can occur whether or not both parents are a part of the immediate family constellation. Some behaviors, in fact, are more likely to occur in the absence of one parent figure.

When a pattern of this nature develops, there is a tendency for the family to identify the dishonest member, for example, as responsible for the bulk of the family's emotional difficulties. The family member so identified is often one of the children. He or she will continue to receive the subtle training already mentioned and may also receive subtle encouragement to develop still other problem behaviors. While the idea that a family would encourage even one problem behavior may appear ridiculous, it can be understood more easily, perhaps, if we view the family as not just a few individuals but a unit. In some cases, the "problem" member is used to establish dramatic "proof" of the family's adequacy in relation to the problem child's inadequacy. Indeed, acceptance comes to depend in large measure upon the child's increasing willingness (conscious or unconscious) to accept the responsibility for family problems in general. Other family members can state with increasing certainty that "we're a great family except for *him*."

As long as the child demonstrates sufficient misconduct to "prove" his responsibility for the bulk of the family problems, this acceptance into the family will be available to him. The child comes to accept such a role as a matter of course. But because families communicate on many different levels, the role of the child with the "identified problem" is often complex and difficult to learn. Meaningful silence is a form of communication as profound (and threatening) as a shouted answer. Each additional child in the family further complicates the communication system: one child merely learns the three systems involving both parents and himself, whereas three children, for example, must interpret ten combinations among five members. The psychological stress mounts as inconsistent (and therefore unpredictable) reactions to other family members emerge.

And yet, the major problem in terms of delinquency is the contradictory or "double" communication that is usually a part of such family dynamics—the verbal "be a good boy" combined with a subtle and nonverbal "be sure to misbehave." Such contradictory messages permit each family member to absolve himself of responsibility for the delinquent's training ("If only you had listened to me") and afford a relative sense of "normality."

In the early stages, contradictory messages are obvious: parental endorsement of honesty followed by punishment for honesty, and so on. Later, the contradiction is difficult to discern, but the very obscurity of the contradiction arouses enough anxiety to induce further misconduct.

Delinquency that is traced to such family dynamics is extremely difficult to treat. The family members tend to sabotage treatment efforts out of their fear of losing the source of their emotional equilibrium should the delinquent be cured. Any plan which threatens to relieve the family of its symbolic scapegoat is apt to cause deep (if unconscious) alarm.

SOCIAL CHANGE

A century ago most young adults were reasonably certain—certain of their status, family, and future. Although the powerful controls that existed were primarily social, the family psychology, too, was influenced by "everybody-knowing-everybody" in small rural communities. This social and family dynamic tended to reinforce feelings of security and predictability and probably provided society with far greater control of delinquency than we can reasonably expect from even the most sophisticated juvenile justice system in this automated, urbanized, cybernated twentieth century.

The urbanization and social change of the Industrial Revolution tended to increase the psychological sources of anxiety and weaken traditional controls; in short, the individual became less secure about his future as modern society impinged upon the family.

THE CULTURAL INFLUENCE

Of course, this is compounded by the frequency with which a mother and father may, for psychological reasons, fear open expression of anger or hostility. Family rules against such expression may suppress not only hostility, but creativity and innovation as well. Family rules may not be explicitly stated; they are often simply understood by those who follow them regularly.

If the family rules differ from what the family says, the cycle discussed earlier begins to emerge. Returning to the example, as children in the family are subtly punished year after year for expression of anything like anger, the emotion of *any* family member who successfully vents hostility may be privately "enjoyed" by other family members who claim to be appalled at how assaultive a delinquent child may be. A younger child born into the family, unaware of the rules against expressing hostility, may fall into the combined role of scapegoat for family problems and source of vicarious satisfactions denied to other family members.

When family dynamics of this nature foster delinquency, they in turn relate to what we will discuss later in this chapter as the "self and other dilemma"—the delinquent's *perception* of himself and others.

EGO-STATE THEORIES

Although modern behavioral science has raised many crucial questions regarding the overall validity of his theory, Sigmund Freud nevertheless devised a useful conceptual tool for accounting for personality disturbances. Freud's *psychoanalysis* is based on his conception of a personality divided into three parts: the *id,* the *ego,* and the *super-ego.* The id is pictured as the source of all basic drives (hunger, sex, and so on). The ego develops through infancy and childhood in a manner that provides the id with a conscious avenue to acquire satisfaction for its drives. The super-ego is equivalent to "conscience" and tends to inhibit the immediate satisfaction of various id drives. The super-ego is the primary consideration when dealing with delinquents.

Using ego-state psychology to explain delinquency hinges upon the notion of conflict, at least in the case of Freud's psychoanalysis. For example, conflict evolves when basic id drives prove incompatible with the super-ego's definition of "civilized existence." Conflict between these two ego states is more subtle, however, when it involves the need for success (id) and the acceptable avenue for success (super-ego). This situation is the basis for a crucial sociological delinquency theory discussed later in this chapter.

In theory, the delinquent is unaware of the *source* of the psychic discomfort that grows out of such ego-state conflicts. He seeks only to reduce the ensuing anxiety (frequently experienced as tension). Theoretically, anxiety (or tension) can be reduced by substituting a fantasy or other unreal mental activity for the conflict (mental illness) or by "acting out" the conflict and thus, to some extent, relieving the anxiety it causes.

For example, the child who has no acceptable means of earning success feels anxious because he has no means of satisfying his id's demand for success. He is trapped between an id commanding him to "do something" and a super-ego saying "but not that." If his parents, at the same time, are giving him nonverbal instructions to be "a problem," he may unconsciously decide that he can resolve the conflict and please his parents by becoming delinquent.

Repression is an extension of this explanation of delinquency. The assumption that id drives are totally incompatible with the laws to which a child is expected to conform leads to the assumption that a child unable to repress these drives will probably become delinquent. If the id is successfully repressed, on the other hand, it continues to seek expression and produces conflict and anxiety. If the child feels guilty about his desires, he may develop a need for punishment in order to restore balance—punishment is available through delinquency.

A modern extension of the ego-state theory is the late Eric Berne's *transactional analysis*.[3] "Transactions" are like psychodynamics, and Berne, like Freud, believed the personality has three components. The child, adult, and parent correspond to the id, ego, and super-ego.

In transactional analysis, delinquency is seen as a game that serves (among other things) to substitute for "real" living. Real living involves *emotional risk* by requiring exposure to *genuine intimacy*. Because intimacy always involves the threat of rejection, some people go to great lengths to avoid it. Games—which can look like real life—reduce the risk of rejection and allow the players to feel comfortable with one another.

Transactional analysis, in addition to the game concept, involves "rackets" and "trading stamps." People can collect two kinds of stamps —brown stamps for bad feelings and gold stamps for good feelings. Brown stamps—for example, insulting remarks from another family

[3] E. Berne, *Games People Play* (New York: Grove Press, 1964).

member—can be saved until the holder "cashes in" the entire book by punching his brother in the nose. Delinquency involving assault and battery is conceivably related to brown stamp collection and the "racket" comes into play when brown stamp collecting is used to justify delinquency.

When delinquency is viewed in the light of a game, it suggests a secret reason for being delinquent and keeping the secret not only from other family members but also from one's own "adult" (ego). The secret reason is the pay-off, which the delinquent usually cannot recognize because it is too subtle and probably, outside of the game context, an unacceptable reward. Typical of many delinquent games are "let's you and him fight," "cops and robbers," "kick me," and "courtroom."

PERSONALITY DISORDER

While many criminologists feel that personality disorders have little or no bearing on delinquency, a few believe that they are a *cause* of certain types of delinquency. The possibility is certainly worth considering.

Mental deficiency, which means that a person's mind has failed to develop to a normal degree, is a subnormality. *Psychosis,* on the other hand, is an abnormality (assuming that psychosis occurs in mentally developed persons). Some psychoses may cause enough mental deterioration to produce mental deficiency, but the mentally deficient individual is not usually psychotic. There are some instances in which mentally deficient children perform delinquent acts. Such delinquency usually can be attributed to a lack of supervision, however. Labelling a mentally deficient child "delinquent" for setting a house on fire is often as meaningless as blaming a three-year-old for the same mistake.

Such personality disorders as psychosis and neurosis are actually related to the ego-state theories already discussed. On a common-sense basis, the mentally ill (psychotic) delinquent will, presumably, stop being a delinquent once his mental illness is cured. However, the personality disorder known as *sociopathy* (sometimes *psychopathy*) is thought by many criminologists to be a direct cause of a great deal of delinquency. A sociopathic personality, defined in terms of ego-state psychology, shows an absence of super-ego (parent) control. Hostility and aggressiveness are directed outward toward others (rather than inward toward oneself) and the sociopath commonly expects immediate satisfaction of all desires. He also demonstrates an inability or unwillingness to form affectional bonds with others.

Criminologists have different opinions on how the sociopathic personality comes into existence, and there is some question whether the psychopath even exists. Even among the most enthusiastic supporters of the sociopathic explanation of delinquency there are differences—possibly based on the extreme complexity of accounting for the origins of such a personality disorder. The most common explanation, however, is that a child raised without any sense of maternal love (or the equivalent) cannot feel threatened by the withdrawal of something that was not granted in the first place. Because alienation from other individuals and society at large holds no fears for the person deprived of loving acceptance from the start, he can ignore the usual implicit controls.

Of course, theoretical explanations of delinquency based on personality disorder are far more varied and complex than this brief overview suggests. But my purpose here has been to present various psychological theories in order to relate them to one another later in the chapter.

Sociological Theories

As with the psychological theories of delinquency, the discussion of sociological explanations of delinquency draws upon an extremely wide range of literature. Although each segment of the literature seeks to isolate a particular concept or facet of delinquency and crime, this discussion draws upon the literature as a whole to provide continuity and balance.

ECOLOGICAL

The ecological theory of delinquency is the premise that delinquency is more apt to occur in some areas than others. Many criminologists cite the work of Clifford R. Shaw as the most significant in this field.[4] Shaw studied delinquency rates recorded in Chicago between 1900 and 1927. Over 55,000 juvenile delinquents were found to live in certain zones of the city. For example, 26.6 percent of male juvenile delinquents came from one zone, whereas virtually no male juvenile delinquency occurred (or at least was recorded) in another zone.

The high delinquency rate in certain zones was accounted for in three ways: an "invasion of industry and commerce" deteriorated some neighborhoods; interest in appearance or moral reputation was subsequently reduced; and, finally, "neighborliness" decreased and the resulting isolation destroyed traditional social controls. Shaw also found that these areas had an influx of immigrants with customs that tended to conflict with local norms. The initial conflict ultimately produced a secondary conflict between first- and second-generation immigrants. Another criminologist, Frederick Thrasher, studied over one thousand Chicago

[4]C. R. Shaw, *Delinquency Areas* (Chicago: University of Chicago Press, 1931).

gangs and found them to be concentrated in factory and railroad centers radiating outward from Chicago's loop district toward the exclusive residential areas.

CULTURAL

Still another theory of delinquent behavior attempts to isolate the culture, or subculture, of the delinquent.[5] There are roughly 160 sociological definitions of *culture,* but as far as delinquency is concerned, *culture* can be thought of as patterns of ideas and values accumulated as a tradition. A *subculture,* then, including a delinquent subculture, is simply a group at variance with the generally accepted patterns, values, and traditional ideas. Of course, most subcultures, while at variance, do not interact or interfere negatively with the overall culture. This is not the case with the delinquency subculture, however.

The cultural theory of delinquency envisions the frustration of lower- and middle-class children as a struggle between *means* and *ends.* That is, when these children competitively struggle for material symbols of wealth, they may find themselves denied access to these symbols because of their subculture. Out of their frustration, they begin searching for alternative (and perhaps illegal) means to the end.

An interesting expansion of Cohen's theory was developed by the noted criminologist, Edwin H. Sutherland.[6] He concluded that some children are excessively exposed to those values that prove conducive to delinquency. A delinquent, therefore, has been *differentially associated* with these values. Of course, Sutherland's theory of *differential association* and other theoretical approaches discussed here are substantially more complex than indicated in this summary.

Certain implications of differential association have been dealt with by another criminologist, Walter Reckless, who was interested in the process by which a child "learns" his culture. Reckless points out that all children, delinquent or not, seem to learn values and other cultural patterns in the same way—only the *content* of what is learned differs.

The problem of attempting to account for delinquency through differential association is that it fails to account for children who are *not* delinquent even though exposed to the same influences. Why do certain people conform to the larger society instead of the immediate environment? This question can be extended to other criminological theories and is the basis for much general criticism. As will be noted later, the answer may hinge partially on individual awareness of others' needs—

[5]A. K. Cohen, *Delinquent Boys* (New York: The Free Press, 1955).
[6]E. H. Sutherland and D. R. Cressey, *Principles of Criminology* (Philadelphia: J. B. Lippincott Co., 1961, 1970).

tion than the family? Given the reality of the other theoretical causes of delinquency, can the family be held accountable at all, and is it possible that virtually all causes of delinquency are potentially correctable within the sphere of influence of the school? Although few sociologists would argue that *all* causes are correctable by the schools, there is increasing, if rather vague, concern with the influence of the school. A later chapter includes discussion of the strategic part played by the school in juvenile justice efforts to cope with delinquency.

The following offers a good summary of the role of social factors in delinquency:

> Some of the features of delinquency that are so pervasive in the United States and that have to be taken for granted as inherent in the idea of delinquency can be absent in other cultures. It is probable that delinquent subcultures have different stresses in different societies and that those could be related to differences in the various social systems of which they are part. This also helps to stress the point that there is nothing inherent in an activity that makes it delinquent. Furthermore, there is the recognition that what is defined as delinquency varies over time. For example, at one time school truancy was defined as a more serious form of delinquency than it is today, . . . [and] one of the most common types of delinquency today did not exist fifty years ago —the stealing of automobiles.[11]

Physiological Theories

Physiological theories about the causes of delinquency revolve around the influence of hereditary physical and biochemical characteristics. Some of these theories are relatively ancient and, by today's standards, may seem naive. However, new interest and research in some of these areas promises to divert attention from the contemporary focus on psychological and sociological causes of delinquency and other deviances.

The part played by heredity remains unclear. Some traits are obviously inherited; scientists are beginning to suspect that we inherit even very subtle components of our total system. But heredity is only one aspect of psysiological theory.

Physiologists, of course, emphasize the role of the body. The possible sociological causes of delinquency are relatively unimportant to them. But M. F. Ashley Montagu, the noted biologist, is among those who seek to combine sociological and physiological theories.[12] He believes that both factors interact to influence behaviors and attitudes.

[11]R. R. Bell, *Social Deviance* (Homewood, Ill.: Dorsey Press, 1971), pp. 307–8.
[12]M. F. Ashley Montagu, "The Biologist Looks at Crime," *The Annals,* 211(1941),45–51.

various levels of awareness may account for varying perceptions
reactions to one's immediate environment.

SOCIAL CAUSES

One of the first beliefs that emerged from early juvenile courts wa
divorce and parental desertion was the cause of most delinquency.
belief no doubt stemmed from the observation that about half (
known juvenile delinquents were from "broken homes." But Sha↑
McKay found that only 42.5 percent of recorded delinquent ch
came from broken homes and interpreted their finding as evidenc
broken homes are a significant but not main cause of delinquenc

Because later studies of 44,000 Philadelphia children showed a d
and continuous decline in the percentage of delinquency among
living with parents, sociologists have tended to focus on the *nat*
parental separation (divorce, desertion, and imprisonment or de
one parent). The definition of *broken home* has been made more e
and the feeling is that the reason for parental separation is more re
than the separation itself.

Still another social variable related to delinquency is *lack of recr*
Studies indicate that delinquents seek exciting diversion. If there :
diversions, delinquency becomes a form of recreation and then a
tion to adult crime.[8]

The national economy also has been cited as a social cause o
quency. The late Paul Tappan, also a criminologist, tended to q
this relationship, however, noting that the overwhelming maj
children from impoverished families do not become involved ii
quency.[9]

THE SCHOOL

"As a principal agency of adolescent socialization, the school m
to foster a commitment to law-abiding behavior among teen-agei
the school *more* responsible for preventing delinquency-pron(

[7]C. R. Shaw and H. McKay, *Juvenile Delinquency and Urban Areas* (Chicago:
of Chicago Press, 1942).

[8]Sheldon Glueck and Eleanor Glueck, *Unraveling Juvenile Delinquency* (l
Commonwealth Fund, 1950).

[9]P. Tappan, *Crime, Justice and Correction* (New York: McGraw-Hill Book
1960), pp. 210–13.

[10]W. E. Schafer, C. Olexa, and K. Polk, "Programmed for Social Class: Tracki
School," in *Schools and Delinquency,* ed. K. Polk and W. Schafer (Englewood
Prentice-Hall, Inc., 1972), pp. 43–44.

This idea might explain why two children brought up in similar environments do not react in the same way. A very simple example of this could be two boys who grow up in a delinquent neighborhood. Both are the oldest of five children; both come from broken homes. One does very well in school; the other does not. One boy earns praise from his teachers and parent and admiration from some of his fellow students for his grades. The other boy earns praise and recognition from his peers for stealing hubcaps. Both are learning their culture, but they are learning those aspects of it for which they can receive recognition.

The boy who does well scholastically has more than one means to an end: he might be able to steal hubcaps as successfully as the other, but he has the alternative of praise for his school work. At the same time, he may value this praise because it is in an area that initially interests him regardless of verbal rewards. When he finishes school, he goes on to college and becomes an electrical engineer. The other boy drops out of school and begins a career in juvenile court.

Sociological factors alone have not determined their futures, although the value attached to "good grades" is of course significant. The fact is that the ability to succeed in school (a relatively high I.Q.) is a physiological (and possibly hereditary) factor that helps determine one's reaction to sociological factors.

BIOCHEMICAL

Those attempting to understand the causes of delinquency through body chemistry found the publication in 1922 of *The Glands Regulating Personality* of considerable value. Since that time, interest in hormones and ductless glands has been expanded to the brain's chemical reactions to emotional stimuli. The discovery that some people have significantly higher and lower levels of these chemicals leads some scientists to suspect that chemical reactions influence individual behavior. There is much interest in the findings and implications of this research.

Research into combinations of X and Y chromosomes indicates that this theoretical explanation, too, may have a significant relation to delinquent and criminal behavior.

PHYSICAL

The nineteenth century Italian physician, Lombroso, devised a system to directly correlate physical features and criminal misconduct. Drawing heavily upon the contemporary belief that there was a relationship between bumps on the head and human personality (phrenology), Lombroso sought to establish "stigmata of degeneration"—physical characteristics that indicated crime and other deviant behaviors.

Ernest Kretchmer developed this concept to the point that, by 1925, his writings formed the foundation of William H. Sheldon's widely recognized system of relating body shape to human behavior. Sheldon classified bodies as *endormorph* (rotund with excessive fatty tissue), *mesomorph* (muscular), or *ectomorph* (lean, angular). According to this theory, the fatter endormorphs are affectionately gregarious and therefore less likely to become delinquent. (Perhaps it was Sheldon who helped define fat people as jolly.) Muscular mesomorphs were considered prone to criminal deviance due to their excessive amount of physical activity, but the lean and often nervous ectomorph was thought too shy to become delinquent.

It is difficult to argue that fat children have a different early life experience than thin children, but it is also difficult to argue that there are no fat or thin delinquents. Although there is general interest in hereditary and physiological factors in delinquency, more of it focuses on the biochemical than the physical.

Delinquency Causes and Perception of Others

Any one category that allegedly causes delinquency is sooner or later questioned because it has "failed" to cause a juvenile who falls within that category to be delinquent.[13] It should be worthwhile, therefore, to consider whether delinquency is caused by a combination of psychological, sociological, and physiological forces.

This possibility was touched on previously, but without any indication of how categories can be combined to produce a consistently workable explanation. The attempt to combine theories must be done on a pragmatic basis—that is, by applying theory in a practical manner. Otherwise, the only consistency will lie in continued discussion and debate, neither of which promises success in coping with delinquency. What is needed is a consistent and practical approach to assessing which cause combines with other specific causes to cause delinquency in particular cases.

The manner in which other people are *perceived,* of course, has great influence on the individual's behavior. For example, if "others" are generally perceived as threatening, various defenses are usually included in the behavior pattern. Self/other perceptions have been discussed briefly, and here the emphasis is on how they relate to other theoretical causes of delinquency.

[13]See, for example, D. C. Gibbons, "Observations on the Study of Crime Causation," *American Journal of Sociology,* Vol. 77, No. 2 (1971), 271.

AWARENESS OF NEEDS

Independent of intelligence, human awareness of needs varies. The teen-age male juvenile may find himself overwhelmed with certain sexual needs which he relates to self. In terms of others, he may be all but unaware of his female peers' needs for warmth, security, affection, and love. If he becomes a sexually assaultive delinquent, the theoretical cause may be a combination of physiological and psychological factors, com-pounded by a (sociological) lack of awareness of others' needs. If this adolescent has a brother who is not sexually aggressive, the difference may be explained in terms of self/other perception. For instance, the brother may be aware of others' needs.

As for the delinquent himself, a slight increase in such awareness might replace sexual assault with sexual seduction. That is, made aware of others' needs in this area, sociological and physiological factors may be combined to obtain sexual gratification by recognizing rather than ignoring the needs of others.

Of course, awareness of needs does not change the *motivational variables* in juvenile delinquency. One young man may steal a car to sell parts for profit and another may steal a car for "thrills" or to impress his girl-friend. While each case is theft, the severity of the two is influenced by motivation. But once the motivational factor has been taken into consideration, there remains the problem of "what-to-do-about-it."

The point is that explaining delinquency accomplishes very little un-less the explanations can be constructively applied to specific individuals and their situation. Awareness of needs is only one example of how theories can be combined and practically applied. Other examples will be discussed in more detail in later chapters.

Summary

After establishing a context in which to deal with both the self-determi-nism on which societal laws are based and the determinism implicit in the theoretical causes of delinquency, we divided these theories into catego-ries (psychological, sociological, or physiological) and discussed them individually. Mention was made of the fallacy in assuming that one theory can account for all delinquent behavior.

As an illustration of how theories can be combined and applied to specific situations, various theories were related to the delinquent's per-ception of others and awareness of their needs. The point was made that theoretical explanations serve little purpose unless they can be used to bring about change in particular and general instances of delinquency.

Questions

1. Compare self-determinism and determinism.
2. Discuss the relationship of law and an orderly society in terms of self-determinism.
3. Explain why theories of delinquency may be considered deterministic.
4. Discuss psychological theories; sociological theories; physiological theories.
5. Contrast any two theories.
6. Relate perception to all three categories.
7. Discuss self/other in terms of theoretical causes of delinquency.
8. Relate awareness of needs to delinquency.
9. Describe how your behavior has been influenced by your parents, your appearance, and your educational experience. Explain how each of these influences fits into one of the categories listed in this chapter.
10. Do you feel that you are *primarily* self-determined or determined by your environment (including family, heredity, neighborhood, and so on)? Explain your answer.
11. Describe your subculture. Does it differ in any respects from what you see as the broader culture? How? How do you differ from others in your subculture?
12. What do *variant* and *deviant* mean to you? Which of the two generally implies the most serious condition? Where is the line drawn between a variant subculture (or personality) and a deviant subculture?

Annotated References

ANDRY, R. G., *Delinquency and Parental Pathology.* London: Methuen, 1960.

BARNES, H. E., and N. K. TEETERS, *New Horizons in Criminology.* Englewood Cliffs, N.J.: Prentice-Hall, Inc., 1960. An excellent survey of the causative theories in crime and delinquency.

BENNETT, J., *Delinquent and Neurotic Children.* New York: Basic Books, Inc., 1960. Case studies in same contexts as many of the explanations of delinquency covered in this chapter.

BERNE, E., *Games People Play.* New York: Grove Press, Inc., 1964.

BRIAR, S., and I. PILIAVIN, "Delinquency, Situational Inducements, and Commitment to Conformity," *Social Problems,* 13 (Summer 1965), 35–45.

BRILL, A., ed., *Basic Writings of Sigmund Freud.* New York: Random House, Inc., 1938.

BURGESS, R. L., and R. L. AKERS, "A Differential Association-Reinforcement Theory of Criminal Behavior," *Social Problems,* 14 (Fall 1966), 128–47.

Buss, A. H., *Psychopathology*. New York: John Wiley & Sons, Inc., 1966.

Cloward, R. A., and L. E. Ohlin, *Delinquency and Opportunity*. New York: The Free Press, Inc., 1960.

Cohen, A. K., *Delinquent Boys*. New York: The Free Press, Inc., 1955.

Downes, D., *The Delinquent Solution*. New York: The Free Press, Inc., 1966.

Ferdinand, T. N., *Typologies of Delinquency*. New York: Random House, Inc., 1966. Comprehensive coverage of the typological approach to delinquency, including some classifications not dealt with in this chapter.

Gibbons, D. C., "Awareness of Others' Needs," *Delinquent Behavior*. Englewood Cliffs, N.J.: Prentice-Hall, Inc., 1970.

_____, "Observations on the Study of Crime Causation," *American Journal of Sociology*, Vol. 77, No. 2 (1971), pp. 262–78. A meaningful critique of theoretical approaches based upon differential association.

Hirschi, T., *Causes of Delinquency*. Berkeley, Calif.: University of California Press, 1969.

Kennedy, D. B., and B. Kennedy, *Applied Sociology for Police*. Springfield, Ill.: Charles C Thomas, Publisher, 1972. Excellent elaboration of sociological concepts referred to in this chapter.

Matza, D., *Delinquency and Drift*. New York: John Wiley & Sons, Inc., 1964.

Phillipson, M., *Sociological Aspects of Crime and Delinquency*. London: Routledge and Kegan Paul, 1971.

Poveda, T. G., "The Image of the Criminal: A Critique of Crime and Delinquency Theories," *Issues in Criminology*, Vol. 5, No. 1 (1970), pp. 59–83. Combines a critique with survey of delinquency theories.

Roebuck, J. B., *Criminal Typology*. Springfield, Ill.: Charles C Thomas, Publisher, 1971. While focused on adult criminality, this innovative approach can also be applied to delinquency.

Satir, V., *Conjoint Family Therapy*. Palo Alto, Calif.: Science and Behavior Books, 1964.

Short, J. T., and T. L. Strodtbeck, *Group Process and Gang Delinquency*. Chicago: University of Chicago Press, 1965.

Shaw, C. R., *Delinquency Areas*. Chicago: University of Chicago Press, 1931.

_____, *The Jack Roller*. Chicago: University of Chicago Press, 1931.

_____, *The Natural History of a Delinquent Career*. Chicago: University of Chicago Press, 1931.

Taft, D. R., *Criminology*. New York: The Macmillan Company, 1956.

Tappan, P. W., *Crime, Justice and Correction*. New York: McGraw-Hill Book Co., 1960. A virtual encyclopedia of both causative theories and their general criminological context.

_____, *Juvenile Delinquency*. New York: McGraw-Hill Book Co., 1959. First of the "classical" compilations of critical thinking on theories of juvenile delinquency.

THRASHER, F. "The Boys Club and Juvenile Delinquency," *American Journal of Sociology,* 42 (1936).

————, *The Gang.* Chicago: University of Chicago Press, 1963.

VOLD, G. B., *Theoretical Criminology.* New York: Oxford University Press, 1958.

VOLLMER, A., *The Criminal.* New York: Foundation Press, 1949.

WOLFGANG, M. E., ed., *Crime and Culture: Essay in Honor of Thorsten Sellin.* New York: John Wiley & Sons, Inc., 1968. An outstanding collection of contributions from many prominent theoreticians in criminology, dealing in depth with the conflict between social and legal norms.

3

Historical Background
of Juvenile Court

Taking the concept of American justice as a whole, probably the least understood segment is the juvenile court, the cornerstone of the juvenile justice system. The problem may arise from the fact that juvenile courts were conceived to serve what amount to two different functions. The first function is *judicial*—a judge's decision as to whether the alleged offense was committed by the minor who appears before the court. The second function is *correctional*—some assessment of social and other factors with an eye to rehabilitating the youth.

It is especially important to understand that the juvenile court is part of the total juvenile justice system, a complex of law enforcement, judging, punishing and helping functions carried on officially and unofficially by a variety of public officers. The several components of this system do not always operate harmoniously with each other for reasons that are, at least in part, attributable to the conflicting goals juvenile justice is designed to serve. It is readily apparent, for example, that providing elements of the good life (educational opportunity, economic security, psychological tranquility, etc.) for a child may sometimes be entirely incompatible with protecting the public from his antisocial depredations. Thus the police may be wholly unsympathetic with the recommendations of the court's psychologist, and vice versa. This clash of individual welfare and public interests occurs, in all stages of the system, but especially in the juvenile court.[1]

A related difficulty is the failure of most citizens to recognize the rationale behind the statutes that have for three-fourths of a century differentiated adult from juvenile justice procedures. Juvenile justice was preceded by the long historical development of the concept of justice itself. Understanding the differences between adult and juvenile court requires some familiarity with this historical background.

The Origins of Justice

Prehistoric man has been pictured as a member of small family groups —groups motivated to remain together for mutual protection from a frequently hostile environment. "It was quite natural for these early communities to select the strongest and most dependable men to stand guard while the other members of the tribe slept. As these early roving bands organized into tribes . . . they began to evolve rules and regulations governing personal and property rights."[2] The authority of the "strongest and most dependable men" may have represented the entire range of justice in prehistoric times. It is probable, however, that the establishment of "rules and regulations" introduced a notion of justice close to that we have today: "the use of authority and power to uphold what is right."[3]

Of course, the definition of "what is right" probably remained in the hands of the "strongest and most dependable" if only because they had the power to uphold whatever form of justice existed. Nevertheless, the relationship between rules, authority, and justice was established. The most consistent aspect of early justice was most likely harsh punishment for transgressions of the group code.

The growth and organization of these tribes affords a gradually greater degree of documentation which in turn permits a more tangible interpretation of the development of justice as a concept. A few thousand years before Christ, Sumerian rulers gradually devised a relatively refined judi-

[1]S. J. Fox, *The Law of Juvenile Courts in a Nutshell* (St. Paul, Minn.: West Publishing Co., 1971), pp. 1–2.

[2]J. L. Sullivan, *Introduction to Police Science* (New York: McGraw-Hill Book Co., 1966), p. 123.

[3]*Webster's New World Dictionary of the American Language,* 2nd ed. (New York: World Publishing Co., 1970).

cial system. In about 2370 B.C., for example, a Sumerian king, Ura-ka-gina, described his efforts to curb oppression of the poor by certain kingdom officials. By recognizing *injustice,* Ura-ka-gina established a principle of justice. Within two centuries, another ruler, Gudea, recorded the suspension of court proceedings on a similar principle. This is believed to be one example of early Babylonian efforts to organize and standardize control of human behavior—still another precept of a judicial system. In 2130 B.C., King Nammu issued a somewhat fragmented but nonetheless organized code of laws—a further example of standardization. Babylonian rulers of the First Amorite dynasty tended to implement and supplement King Nammu's code, and, in the centuries that followed, a system of "justice via precedent" (similar to our common law) emerged.

But it was the Babylonian king, Hammurabi, who provided what most historians agree is the cornerstone of the judicial system as we know it. The Great Code of Hammurabi specified offenses and accompanying penalties, in the most sophisticated attempt at standardization of the time.

Although the penalties of the Hammurabian Code remained as brutal as those of the extremely severe *lex talionis* (an earlier unwritten code), the profound influence of the concept that "the crime must fit the offense" can not be overestimated. The Hammurabian Code was written over one thousand years before Mosaic Law and, for many centuries, was a model for the judicial system of many cultures.

However, many of its salient features were lost for a few hundred years following the decline of the Roman Empire. Certain developments in France indirectly influenced the justice concept in the late Dark Ages and immediately after. But it is to feudal England that the American judicial system—and particularly juvenile justice—must trace its heritage.

The English Influence

While the context for juvenile justice was slow to evolve, the principle on which the first American juvenile court was founded can be traced deep into English history. *Parens patriae* is the principle that the king is, by definition, the *parent of his country.* He is the "father" who determines family rules, budget limitations, family activities, *and* the disciplinary action for violation of family rules. But because the king's "family" was an entire nation, he required assistance in the administration of these affairs.

The earliest effort to provide this assistance was the Court of Chancery, or "equity court," which handled, among others, the problems of dependent (but not criminal) children.

CHANCERY COURT AND *PARENS PATRIAE*

While the chancery court did not separate adult from juvenile justice in all cases, it nevertheless established the concept of individualized justice. A great deal of time was to pass, however, before this concept would be extended to children accused of crime.

Perhaps the modified juvenile justice system was handicapped by such "refinements" as the "benefit of clergy" rule, which permitted men of the cloth to claim exemption from punishment for crimes. This was individualized justice carried to an unjust extreme. In any event, the Courts of Chancery, a result of the *parens patriae* philosophy, where the ultimate basis of the first American juvenile court.

American Development

So *direct* was the influence of the English chancery courts on the first American juvenile court that it might be conceived of as an actual transfer. This transfer of the English chancery court to American juvenile justice was not only direct but extremely swift by historical standards—at least swift once underway.

As early as 1861, Chicago children were being separated from adults in the criminal court process. An 1869 Massachusetts law established an appointed position to serve on what was then called the State Board of Charity, the appointed person to represent children under sixteen in criminal court. The following year, Massachusetts passed another law establishing "sessions for juvenile offenders," clearly delineating the distinction between adults and juveniles on virtually the same basis as the English chancery courts. In that same year, New York passed a law prohibiting the confinement of children with adult offenders—a commonly accepted principle in modern criminal justice but thought radical at the time.

It would be difficult, if not impossible, to estimate the significance of the Chicago juvenile court in terms of children's rights or in terms of institutionalizing the concept of pertinent justice with the court system.

The principle of "petitioning the court on behalf of the child" became law in 1893 in Indiana and covered not only neglected but delinquent children as well. Procedurally, this Indiana law empowered the circuit court to consider the petition (as opposed to a criminal court complaint) and, if judged true, place the child with the Board of Children's Guardians,[4] instead of in prison.

[4]C. E. Reasons, "Guilt: Procedural Change and Substantive Effect," *Crime and Delinquency*, Vol. 16, No. 2 (1970), 164.

EARLY JUVENILE COURTS

The Juvenile Court Act of Illinois, passed in April 1899, established a statewide juvenile court system. The first juvenile court was formed in Cook County (Chicago), Illinois, within a few months of passage of the act. Under the new law (and hastily devised amendments) all children (neglected, "incorrigible," and delinquent) involved with courts came under a single jurisdiction. This first juvenile court, as did others after it, conducted closed hearings (public not admitted) and kept confidential court records. Twenty-five years after Illinois made juvenile court mandatory, two states still had not established such a system for their youth.[5]

One of the first distinctions between juvenile and adult court was the language. *Criminal complaint* was replaced by *juvenile court petition; arraignment* was replaced by *initial hearings; conviction* was replaced by *finding-of-involvement;* and *sentence* by *disposition.* To buttress the distinction further, the physical surroundings were less imposing and "the goals were to investigate, diagnose, and prescribe treatment, not to adjudicate guilt or fix blame."[6] While informality was emphasized, the juvenile court judge nevertheless presided and matters were dealt with in a serious manner. The basic distinction, however, was that between adult responsibility and juvenile accountability (see Chapter 1). From the outset there was a conspicuous effort to simultaneously minimize the authoritarian atmosphere and emphasize various degrees of accountability for law violation.

Insofar as the operation of these early juvenile courts was concerned, there is little doubt that the English chancery courts were a significant influence: "As *parens patriae,* the state, substituting for king, invested the juvenile court with the power to act as parent of the child. The judge was to assume a fatherly role, protecting the juvenile in order to cure and save him. The juvenile court withheld from the child the procedural safeguards granted to adults because it viewed him as having the right to custody rather than the right to liberty, and juvenile proceedings were civil, not criminal."[7]

AMERICAN INNOVATION

One of the earliest American modifications of the chancery court concept occurred ten years after the inception of the first juvenile court. The

[5]T. Rubin and J. T. Smith, *The Future of the Juvenile Court: Implications for Correctional Manpower and Training* (Washington, D.C.: Joint Commission on Correctional Manpower and Training, 1968), p. 1.

[6]The President's Commission on Law Enforcement and Administration of Justice, *Task Force Report: Juvenile Delinquency and Crime* (Washington, D.C.: U.S. Gov't. Printing Office, 1967), p. 3.

[7]C. E. Reasons, "Guilt," p. 164.

Chicago juvenile court began to move away from concern with the nature of the offense to concern for why it had been committed. Research by Dr. William Healy first indicated that delinquency could have many causes which vary in individual cases. Called by some "the clinical approach" to juvenile delinquency,[8] this concept continues to be developed and expanded. (The implications of and impact on juvenile justice of the clinical approach will be elaborated in later chapters.) At the time this approach was introduced, it was met with great enthusiasm and sympathy by the general public.

The Illinois Juvenile Court Act of 1899 was one of the first reflections of a movement beginning to be felt throughout American society. Children, who had been victimized by the Industrial Revolution and urbanization, among other economic and sociological phenomena, became the object of widespread concern. This concern was past due and certainly justified, but was perhaps sentimentalized out of guilt that children's rights had been callously ignored for far too long.

The clinical philosophy was not applied only to juvenile justice. It extended into many aspects of child welfare. But in relation to the justice system, social and psychological conditions were so emphasized that court interest in the offenses themselves was all but eliminated. Consequently, juvenile court law virtually eliminated the possibility that children under a certain age could even be held accountable—a substantially more liberal view than that currently accepted.

This approach was the basis of the court's claim to responsibility and authority for protecting the child. Protection included custody and discipline but emphasized all possible efforts to approximate that which should have been given by the minor's parents.

Interest in and enthusiasm for the clinical approach continued to influence and modify juvenile court procedures, and a concept originating with chancery court received correspondingly greater emphasis. *Equity* is a principle of the juvenile court which allows a certain flexibility in the disposition, or settlement, of a case. For example, the penal codes of most state jurisdictions prescribe a sentence of some kind for a particular criminal act. In juvenile court, however, the judge may choose the clinical approach and assign no penalty with the defense that this course is most equitable. The role of the state or the court as protector of the minor is, of course, strengthened under the equity concept. And the philosophical boundaries of the juvenile court, of necessity broader than that of the criminal court, are further extended by the clinical approach.

The inclusion of "wayward youth" (previously described as predelinquents) no doubt facilitated the liberal interpretation of the role of juvenile court. The practice of combining different juvenile problems under

[8]E. Eldefonso, *Law Enforcement and the Youthful Offender* (New York: John Wiley & Sons, Inc., 1972), p. 190.

a single jurisdiction has resulted in a variety of procedures for handling these problems and a variety of methods for referring children to juvenile court. But the principles established by *parens patriae* and the chancery courts have prevailed, and the court assumes parental responsibility for a child whenever a petition is found to be true and the child is declared a court ward.

Photo by Charles Tado, County of Santa Clara, California

Operations

A fairly consistent standard for the juvenile court began to develop with the adoption of the clinical approach. The U.S. Children's Bureau outlines the following court standards:

1. Courts have broad jurisdiction in cases of youth under eighteen years of age who require court action or protection because of their acts or circumstances.
2. Judges are chosen because of their special qualifications for juvenile court work: legal training, understanding of social problems, and knowledge of child development.
3. Court hearings should be private, rather than public.

4. The court's procedure should be as informal as possible and should still conform to the rules of evidence.

5. Detention should be in separate detention facilities for youth and should be used only if the following conditions exist:

   a. The minor is in need of proper and effective parental care or control and has no parent, guardian, or responsible relative; or has no parent, guardian, or responsible relative willing to exercise, or capable of exercising, such care or control; or has no parent, guardian, or responsible relative actually exercising such care or control.

   b. The minor is destitute, is not provided with the necessities of life, or is not provided with a home or suitable abode.

   c. The minor is provided with a home which us unfit by reason of neglect, cruelty, or depravity of either of his parents, or of his guardian or other persons in whose custody or care he is.

   d. Continued detention of the minor is a matter of immediate and urgent necessity for the protection of the minor or the person or property of another.

   e. The minor is likely to flee the jurisdiction of the court.

   f. The minor has violated an order of the juvenile court.

   g. The minor is physically dangerous to the public because of a mental or physical deficiency, disorder, or abnormality.

6. The juvenile court should have a qualified probation staff, with limited caseloads.

7. Resources should be available for individualized and specialized treatment; for example, psychological, psychiatric, and medical facilities.

8. There should be an adequate record-keeping system which provides for both social and legal records that are safeguarded from indiscriminate public inspection.

9. Youth brought before the juvenile court for criminal acts should not be defined as criminals, but rather as delinquents.

The availability of qualified probation staff and resources for treatment will be the subjects of later chapters. For, while the unqualified acceptance of the clinical approach will be questioned, the need for treatment (clinical or not) remains a concern of the juvenile court.

Although I have traced the historical background of a concept, the *operation* of juvenile justice has been developed in a relatively short span of time. It should not be surprising that, after only seventy-five years, juvenile court procedures continue to be refined and developed. Because the operation is historically new, such expressions of concern as the following should be anticipated:

The juvenile court system has come under heavy criticism in the past several years. Most of the criticism has been well-meaning and perhaps stems from the same idealistic motivation and real concern for children which brought the court into being. Regrettably, too few of the court's critics have possessed an understanding of the juvenile court process. No one would seriously question that society must have some agency concerned with the criminal law violations and the aberrant behavior of children. It is difficult to conceive of such an agency being anything other than an integral part of the administration of justice. Therefore, before contemplating any sweeping changes in the juvenile court system, a realistic appraisal of the court's processes is absolutely essential. Certainly all criticism of the court must be constructive and be directed toward a goal we all share—a workable system to provide requisite care for troubled children which will lead them to healthy and productive adulthood.[9]

Viewed from the perspective of developing an effective *system* of juvenile justice in America, this sort of inquiry is both essential and constructive.

Summary

This chapter introduced the juvenile court as possibly the least understood segment of American justice. The history of the concept of justice was presented as a background for the development of juvenile justice in America. Prehistoric and early Babylonian influences were considered, and the Code of Hammurabi was cited as a crucial element in the evolution of the judicial system. Feudal England, and *parens patriae* and equity, hallmarks of the early English chancery courts, were cited as influences on the first American juvenile court, founded in Chicago in 1899.

A significant American innovation—the clinical approach—was discussed in terms of its impact on juvenile court procedures. Its influence, combined with that of the English chancery court, resulted in the evolution of American juvenile court procedures, which were acknowledged to vary, within a broad standard, from state to state.

Questions

1. Discuss prehistoric "justice."
2. Relate early Sumerian justice to the standardization of offenses.
3. Discuss the relationship of standardization of offenses to a concept of justice.
4. Elaborate the significance of the Hammurabian Code.
5. Discuss the significance of the early English chancery court to the early American juvenile court.

[9]W. G. Whitlatch, "Toward an Understanding of the Juvenile Court Process," *Juvenile Justice,* Vol. 23, No. 3 (1972), 2.

6. Relate *parens patriae* to the first American juvenile court.

7. Elaborate on the introduction of the clinical approach into American juvenile courts.

Annotated References

ELDEFONSO, E., *Youth Problems and Law Enforcement.* Englewood Cliffs, N.J.: Prentice-Hall, Inc., 1972. This small volume contains a great deal of information regarding the youthful offender. It is a handy little reference.

FOX, S. J., *The Law of Juvenile Courts in a Nutshell.* St. Paul, Minn.: West Publishing Co., 1971. An excellent survey of the structure and venue of juvenile court operations.

"Juvenile Due Process in the Lower Court," *The Journal of Criminal Law, Criminology and Police Science,* Vol. 62, No. 3 (1971), 335–49. A great deal of information regarding some upper court decisions on juvenile court law.

MARTIN, J. L., and J. P. FITZPATRICH. *Delinquent Behavior: A Redefinition of the Problem.* New York: Random House, Inc., 1965. A fine resource; pages 35–37 elaborate on the use of punishment in the evolution of justice.

NATHANSON, N. L., "Jury Trials—Juvenile Court," *The Journal of Criminal Law, Criminology and Police Science,* Vol. 62, No. 4 (1971), 497–504. This is an excellent review of Supreme Court decisions that have shaped recent changes in juvenile court law.

POUND, R., "The Juvenile Court and the Law," *Crime and Delinquency,* Vol. 10, No. 4 (1964), 490–504. A philosophical perspective on juvenile court law.

————, "The Juvenile Court in the State Service," *Crime and Delinquency,* Vol. 10, No. 4 (1964), 516–31.

THE PRESIDENT'S COMMISSION ON LAW ENFORCEMENT AND ADMINISTRATION OF JUSTICE, *Task Force Report: Juvenile Delinquency and Youth Crime.* Washington, D.C.: U.S. Gov't. Printing Office, 1967. Covers the history, philosophy, legal and social implications of delinquency.

REASONS, C. E., "Guilt: Procedural Change and Substantive Effect," *Crime and Delinquency,* Vol. 16, No. 2 (1970). An exceptionally well-written elaboration of the relation between court philosophy and impact on procedural matters.

SLOANE, H. W., "The Juvenile Court: An Uneasy Partnership of Law and Social Work," *Journal of Family Law,* Vol. 5, No. 2 (1965). The relationship between law and social work is explored in the context of "clinical philosophy."

WESTBOOK, E., *"Mens Rea* in the Juvenile Court," *Journal of Family Law,* Vol. 5, No. 2 (1965).

WHITLATCH, W. G., "Toward an Understanding of the Juvenile Court Process," *Juvenile Justice,* Vol. 23, No. 3 (Nov. 1972).

4

The System
of Juvenile Justice

One of the most valid criticisms of American criminal justice is that in many ways it is fragmented to the point of being a non-system. The same criticism of the juvenile justice subsystem of criminal justice may be equally valid.

A system can be thought of as a means of organizing and processing input in order to attain specific ends. Below is a simple diagram of this concept:

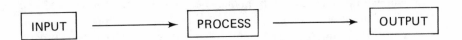

Input, in the case of juvenile justice, is certain law violations defined as delinquency; process is the activities of police, probation, juvenile court, and juvenile corrections; and output is the collective (and, therefore, systematically related) success of these processes.

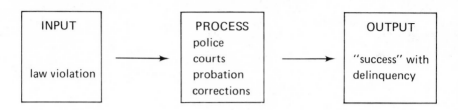

The same illustration can clarify any one of the subsystems involved in the juvenile justice subsystem—for example, the probation subsystem.

Diagrams do not simplify the system but should help to simplify our *concept* of the system. Juvenile justice, of course, is only one part of the entire criminal justice system, and, in this broader context, juvenile justice is actually a subsystem.

Fragmentation can occur at any point during input, process, or output, and it can occur at all points simultaneously. But, in most instances, fragmentation serious enough to merit concern occurs during the process. Since the juvenile justice process is made up of the activities of police, probation, court, and corrections, there are numerous opportunities for fragmentation (refer to the flow charts on pages 45 and 46 to visualize further possibilities for fragmentation):

1. Police take *all* violators into custody when juvenile detention facilities are geared for only the detention of serious delinquents.
2. Probation and courts return dangerous delinquents too quickly to the community without regard for the public safety sought by the police subsystem.
3. Correctional institutions do not adequately prepare their delinquent charges to return to the community (that is, priority is given to an "orderly institution" instead of "rehabilitation"), perpetuating the delinquency confronting the police.

Fragmentation can also be understood in terms of *efficiency* and *effectiveness.* Let us assume that every subsystem of juvenile justice (police, probation, and so on) is operating efficiently. Will juvenile justice be effective; that is, will the process have the desired output?

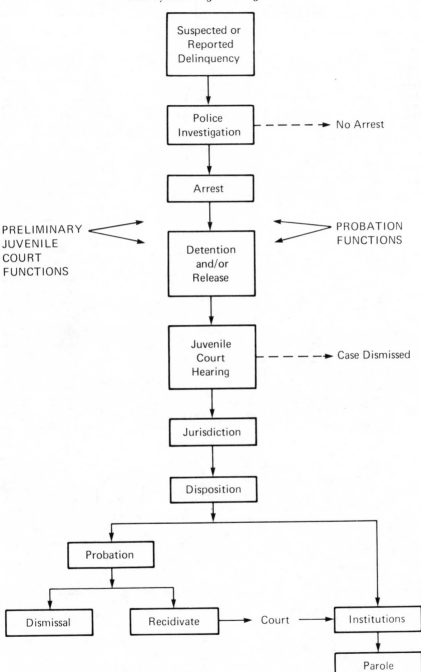

Figure 4–1

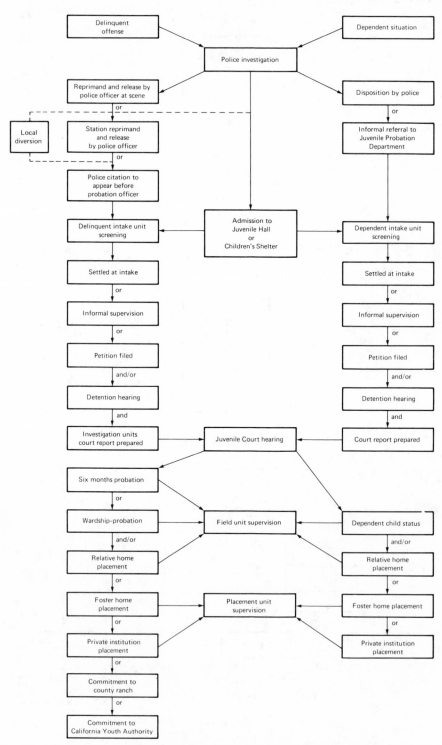

Figure 4-2. Actual Example of Juvenile Justice Flow Process

A car is also a system. The subsystems of a car may operate efficiently —the engine may be tuned, the power column may be aligned, etc. If the only purpose of the car system is the efficient operation of its subsystems, we can be pleased. However, the output goal of this system might be the movement of passengers. If the car becomes stuck in the mud, the passengers will not be moved and the system will not achieve its desired output. No matter how *efficiently* the wheels spin, the passengers in this subsystem are not moving. The *efficient* car is not *effective.*

With reference to the juvenile justice system, too, *efficiency* can be obtained without *effectiveness.* Juvenile justice subsystems can process delinquent children very efficiently but in such a way that there is no *effective* overall reduction in delinquency.

Cause and Effect

Ideally, of course, a system is both efficient and effective. But when this is not the case, attention should be directed to what makes the system "keep going." If a community has an efficient government, it has a community organizational system. The system is a consistent chain of causes and effects. The consistency of the chain means that governmental services are provided on a predictable basis. Desirable results are produced on a "self-adjusting" basis. Complaints about excessive fire or crime are not required before the government system takes action. Complaints about inadequate water supplies are not necessary to get the government to explore these system needs. Sensitivity to the problem for which the system is intended insures consistent and proper adjustment to the output of the system. In an effective system of community organization, licensing, regulating, and similar difficulties are anticipated when possible and dealt with on a cause-and-effect basis even when impossible to anticipate. This interaction of causes and effects produces the desired results in an effective system of government.

In terms of the juvenile justice system, an increase in drug abuse referrals (cause) might reduce police emphasis on car thefts (effect). But compare the community organization with its sensitivity to social changes to the juvenile justice system which adjusts the system after the complaint. Also, consider the effect on the overall system if any subsystem functions so independently (if efficiently) that it is not directly related to the system's output. The fire department which is completely independent of the water department may find insufficient water with which to fight fires.

The system that anticipates change and problems and adjusts itself to change clearly produces better results with less effort. The individual functions of police, probation, juvenile court, and juvenile corrections, which serve a common goal, can—through sensitivity to change and the *direction* of change—function *systematically*. Like the community organization system, the juvenile justice system finds that social change, legal change, and economic change, among others, impinge directly upon its subsystems in a variety of ways.

FLEXIBILITY

The demands made by change call for flexibility. A brief glimpse at the significance of change (especially social change) might illustrate the need for a flexible juvenile justice system. Tremendously oversimplified, the history of man might be thought of in terms of thousands of years of farming followed by two hundred years of an industrial and technical revolution. Against a background of suddenly accelerated change, man faces an uncertain future. The ever-accelerating pace affects nearly everyone in our society. The juvenile justice system, like any other, needs incredible flexibility in order to survive as an *effective* societal force.

But flexibility, in a system involving millions of interactions, can easily become chaotic disorganization. Knowing which interaction is significant and the degree of its significance—to what degree it affects other subsystems and the overall juvenile justice system—is extremely important. An effective juvenile justice system distinguishes between a number of variables, not least of which is the relative significance of certain interactions which may indicate the need for additional adjustments to "temperature changes" in society's delinquency problems. Finally, the effective juvenile justice system focuses on output (goals); its processes do not serve to perpetuate the system but to coordinate subsystems in terms of output.

Summary

This chapter introduced juvenile justice as a system and as a subsystem of the larger criminal justice system. Both juvenile and adult justice have been criticized as so fragmented that they cannot properly be regarded as systems. The activities of juvenile justice were sketched in terms of *input, process,* and *output,* however, and a distinction was made between the *efficient* system and the *effective* system.

Subsystems of juvenile justice are the police, the court, and the probation and correction departments. Key variables among these subsystems are the responses to cause and effect. Output, or the goal, was emphasized as a factor crucial to the success of any system.

Questions

1. Discuss *process* in terms of the flow chart (Figure 4-2).
2. Where would *output* be placed on the flow chart?
3. Distinguish between system efficiency and system effectiveness.
4. Discuss causes and effects in terms of relationships among juvenile justice subsystems.
5. In your opinion, which is the more important function of a system—*process* or *output?* Explain why one is more and the other less important.
6. From what you know of juvenile justice, do you think the system produces only positive output? Explain your answer.

Annotated References

CICOUREL, A. V., *The Social Organization of Juvenile Justice.* New York: John Wiley & Sons, Inc., 1968. Good sociological context for the system of juvenile justice.

ELDEFONSO, E., *Youth Problems and Law Enforcement.* Englewood Cliffs, N.J.: Prentice-Hall, Inc., 1972. An excellent survey of the police subsystem in juvenile justice and five perspectives on juvenile court.

HOWLETT, F. W., and H. HURST, "A Systems Approach to Comprehensive Criminal Justice Planning," *Crime and Delinquency,* Vol. 17, No. 4 (1971), 345–61. Outstanding presentation of the systems concept within criminal justice; extremely eloquent argument against continued fragmentation of crime and delinquent program effort.

KENNEY, J. P., and D. G. PURSUIT, *Police Work with Juveniles and the Administration of Juvenile Justice.* Springfield, Ill.: Charles C Thomas, Publisher, 1972.

THE PRESIDENT'S COMMISSION ON LAW ENFORCEMENT AND ADMINISTRATION OF JUSTICE, *Task Force Report: Juvenile Delinquency and Youth Crime.* Washington, D.C.: U.S. Gov't. Printing Office, 1967. The first two chapters document the fragmentation of the juvenile justice system.

SCHODERBEK, P. P., ed., *Management Systems.* New York: John Wiley & Sons, Inc., 1967. An encyclopedic review of the systems approach.

5

Diversion, Prevention, and Control

Potential and actual delinquency, caused by a variety of more or less destructive elements and manifested in a variety of minor and major offenses, must be dealt with in a manner reflecting its complexity. Fortunately, this necessity is realized, in varying degrees, by nearly all police departments. The formality of the procedure and the result will vary according to department size and location. But whether it is the "local cop" who gives a first offender a fatherly warning or a juvenile officer in the large city who refers the adolescent to the Youth Service Bureau (YSB), there is almost universal recognition of mitigating circumstances and individual problems.

The emphasis in this chapter will be on the crucial role played by one of the juvenile justice subsystems—the police—in the diversion, prevention, and control of delinquency. One might argue that, overall, the police are no more crucial than, for example, the juvenile court or probation subsystems. But, in the overwhelming majority of cases, it is the police who *select* the delinquent juveniles with whom the other juvenile justice subsystems will work.

Moreover, if a juvenile is to be detained, police discretion determines which law violation will be charged. Indeed, most police have the power to determine if *anything* will be charged—regardless of the offenses which may have been committed.

Depending on the nature of the offense, number of previous offenses, and similar factors, one of three approaches can be taken: diversion, prevention, or control. *Diversion* applies primarily to the predelinquent —that is, the juvenile who exhibits the first signs of a delinquent behavior pattern. His problem or offense, usually minor, has come to the attention of the police. In their estimation, he will benefit most if further diverted from contact with delinquency and the juvenile justice system. *Prevention* measures apply to both the predelinquent and the delinquent. These measures are generally undertaken by the police, although, as I will explain later, community participation is extremely important. When diversion and prevention have failed, *control* temporarily isolates the juvenile from the community and further opportunity for delinquency.

Except for a fairly widespread practice of separating the community (or public) relations officers from the rest of the juvenile department, all juvenile officers generally handle diversion, prevention, and control. This practice insures a consistent, reliable, and systematic departmental approach. Diversion, prevention, and control are, in some instances, arbitrary categories. If the department were forced into assigning cases to one of three categories, there is the potential for considerable overlap and inefficient use of manpower. In the small department without a separate juvenile bureau, of course, all officers handle all categories of juvenile offense. For the purposes of this book, however, diversion, prevention, and control in most cases will be treated as three distinct procedures.

Diversion

Police efforts to divert juveniles from the juvenile justice system are, of course, selective—not all children who come to their attention should be diverted to other resources in the community. Many juveniles require the overall services of juvenile court, probation, and even corrections. Our concern here, however, is the juvenile who does not appear likely to gain from further experience in a system geared primarily to the delinquent.

The manner in which juveniles become delinquent varies widely and may not begin with actual delinquency. Being beyond parental control, for example, falls into the category of offenses that would not be offenses if committed by an adult. Why a child should be considered delinquent for such an "offense" lies in the frequent requirement that police must intervene in these cases.

Faced with what often appears to be an unsolvable family problem, many police feel that the only alternative is to refer the child to the same juvenile justice system that serves the other juvenile problems they encounter. Not surprisingly, children whose delinquency has been minimal (or even nonexistent) prior to such an encounter with juvenile justice (and other delinquents), may learn behavior that proves of far more concern to police than the original problem.

The possibility, and the frequent probability, that the influence of delinquents will prevail, underlies the rationale for considering many beyond-controls predelinquent. As such, and to the best interest of all concerned, they can be diverted from the juvenile justice system. "The policeman often dispenses monitory justice (warnings). Typically he settles and decides more violations than he takes into court. He 'judges' thousands of cases every year . . . petty thefts, breaking windows, and starting fires."[1] These decisions divert numerous juveniles and make up a significant amount of police contact with minor children.

However, the ultimate value of diversion is not always clear to the officer who, aware that adolescents are responsible for a disproportionate amount of crime, assumes that exposure to the juvenile justice system will "cure" the early offender. The public, too, could be more aware of the value of diversion.

Public Awareness

Most authorities on juvenile justice agree that there is a wide gap between the reality and the public understanding of diversion.

> The general public must simply be made to understand that it gains neither protection nor security from a punitive and repressive system of dealing with juvenile delinquency. Probation officers who recommend—and lawyers who support without challenge—the detention or commitment of a youngster to an institution where he will be preyed upon, and in other ways made bitter rather than better, are serving neither the public nor their young client. Judges who permit detention in substandard facilities and who commit to ill-equipped and understaffed training schools clearly violate the juvenile or family court laws of every state, which require the court to see that the child shall receive the care, custody, and treatment that he should have received in his own home.[2]

[1]C. B. Vedder, *The Juvenile Offender: Perspective and Readings* (New York: Doubleday & Company, Inc., 1954), p. 193.

[2]M. G. Rector, "Statement Before the U.S. Senate Subcommittee to Investigate Juvenile Delinquency," *Crime and Delinquency,* Vol. 16, No. 1 (1970), 93.

The public, of course, has its own interests. Unless it understands the realities, diversion takes on the appearance of "coddling." A child who has been involved in a first minor offense is free to pursue a life of crime (and, in the public view, will do just that) because the police choose not to punish him. Also, any predelinquent children who are diverted from the juvenile justice system become an indirect responsibility of the community. There is some natural and, to a degree, logical resentment of what appears to be police unwillingness to assume control.

Much public concern can be dealt with through informational programs. For example, the popular misconception that adult crime is the mature form of juvenile delinquency can be disproved: most juvenile delinquents do not become adult criminals. The public needs to be reassured, however, that the police can discriminate between the potential adult criminal and the "temporary" delinquent. Diversion is not a fancy name for irresponsibility but an authentic effort to decrease delinquency.

Alternatives

Thousands of delinquents are diverted *from* the juvenile justice system. Where are they diverted *to*? No one can be diverted from one path unless he has an alternative route, and the provision of alternatives to delinquency is a serious and complex business. Predelinquents need social and job referral services, information and counseling centers, and community recreational facilities. If such services are not provided, the police have only two alternatives: return the child to an apparently problematic environment or involve him in the juvenile justice system. Neither is likely to be constructive.

There is and need not be a standard approach to developing community alternatives. There are, however, some standard factors involved which may influence the direction of such programs as the following:

Santa Clara County Predelinquent Diversion Project:
Quarterly Report for July, August, and September, 1972:
Program Overview

In essence, this is a demonstration project to determine the alternative to referring the predelinquent child to the juvenile justice system. . . . Promptly closing "official" predelinquent cases requires considerable effort. The point made here, however, is that the Juvenile Court process was not found to be necessary in nearly three quarters of the cases referred.

It is the thesis of this project that law enforcement personnel can provide the services necessary in predelinquent matters *before* "official referral" is made. This premise is based on the belief that sufficient community alternatives can be developed through coordinated efforts. Obviously, a significant percentage of predelinquent cases investigated by police are not officially referred; therefore, diversion is a continuing program.

Hopefully, this will put increased emphasis on family responsibility which will reduce the involvement of law enforcement in family matters of any kind. The absence of official records for what are customarily family problems is a further advantage.[3]

The following commentary clarifies the general context in which this and similar programs are conceived:

Alternatives to criminalization should be developed for use from the time an illegal act occurs to adjudication. These procedures should be preferred over traditional punitive measures for those offenders who do not present a serious threat to others.

Diversion programs should be a part of the same planning process that is performed for the rest of the criminal justice process, and particularly corrections. . . . As with other correctional programs, systematic review and evaluation of policies and procedures should be provided for. The community should be represented in the planning process, and the community resources that may be used in the program identified and enlisted. . . .

Most of the diversion processes operating today are informal and are not mandated by statutes. On the contrary, they are the result of ambiguities in existing legislation as well as the broad administrative discretion of officials administering criminal justice. The discretionary decisions are influenced by a variety of factors, but of most importance is the scarcity of system resources. Diversion often occurs because of the pragmatic and pressing realization that there are not enough resources to handle the potential, if not actual, caseload. . . .

If diversion programs are to perform as they are intended then the decisions of those referring to these programs must be subject to review and evaluation. In a similar vein, decision makers cannot have the freedom to make referrals outside of their system unless they have necessary information about alternative programs and the authority to make decisions referring cases out of the system. Guidelines outline the information necessary to meet the requirements of both of these conditions.[4]

THE YOUTH SERVICE BUREAU

A community-based center that affords direct services to youth and their families is most promising. Such centers can bring the police, as consultants on delinquency and delinquency prevention, into a participating

---

[3]Santa Clara County Predelinquent Diversion Project, "Program Overview," *Quarterly Report,* July–September, 1972.

[4]Law Enforcement Assistance Administration, *Working Papers for the National Conference on Criminal Justice* (Washington, D.C., 1973), p. C-77.

relationship with other community agencies. Perhaps the best known program today is the Youth Service Bureau. In the early stages of development around the country, YSB's are anything but uniform in program, formation, or funding. For the most part, federal or state funds subsidize a variety of YSB program proposals which generally focus on a team approach.

Although there are differing views on who should administer the YSB (police, juvenile court, juvenile probation, social welfare, or one of many private social agencies) there is little disagreement on the potential value of the agency. And most authorities on juvenile justice also agree that, whether or not the police administer the YSB, their participation is a definite asset.

Successful staffing includes police, probation, social work, and mental health personnel working as a team to provide youth and family services and involves a wide range of community resources. In such a context, the police officer applies his law enforcement experience to the mutual concerns of youth, their families, and the juvenile justice system. Combined with the expertise of other YSB staff, the program offers convincing evidence to the community that delinquency is not the problem of police alone.

Of course the YSB is completely compatible with such law enforcement programs as PAL, but the primary goal is the provision of counseling and guidance services and the development of other community alternatives. The overlap between YSB and police prevention programs is fortunate and in no way reduces the priority of diversion. "Diversion is 'an opportunity, not a solution.' It is a concept that seems to carry with it 'the possibility of reallocating existing resources for programs that promise greater success in bringing about correction and the social restoration of offenders.' "[5]

Prevention

Successful prevention, like diversion, cannot be accomplished by the police alone. A community must acknowledge that much, if not most, of juvenile delinquency is spawned in youthful spheres of influence that are not always susceptible or accessible to the influence of police. This is only one of numerous limitations on the police role in prevention. Police influence in slum areas is also restricted by the inability of even the most successful prevention programs to change a wide range of social and economic conditions.

But, restricted or not, police influence can and must be used to prevent

[5]R. Barron, F. Feneey, and W. Thornton, "Preventing Delinquency through Diversion," *Federal Probation,* Vol. 37, No. 1 (1973), 18.

the alienation of youth. Police influence cannot reduce the impact of over-crowded, inferior housing; neighborhood violence and criminality; and the hopelessness with which many adolescents confront the future. But the police could "model" the concept of delinquency prevention in such a manner that other community influences would be moved to participate.

The slum is not the only area of concern. Schools and recreation areas, whether located in a poor or wealthy district, can be centers of delinquency. Even such single entertainment events as a rock concert at times generate severe delinquency. Prevention is obviously desirable from a law enforcement viewpoint and therefore worth all possible police involvement.

Prevention, then, becomes a matter of exerting whatever influence is possible to modify or change those conditions that relate to delinquency. In some instances, police influence at best may modify some of the impact of unfortunate conditions by modeling the concern necessary to stimulate other community influences. In the case of youth entertainment and recreation, police influence may be the key to modifying or completely changing the conditions associated with delinquency. And, of course, there is a wide range of possible influence in areas other than slums and recreation centers.

It seems reasonable to assume that the overwhelming majority of law enforcement officers would agree that preventing juvenile offenses is ultimately more effective than dealing with offenses after they have been committed. But there are other considerations:

> The desire to prevent crime is commendable. Unfortunately, it is much like being patriotic or standing for virtue: how does one go about it, and by what objective criteria may success be measured? . . . When the patrolmen leave roll call and get in their cars ... they go to their patrol districts in order to make themselves readily available for call within a specific geographic area. Since the officer spends a great deal of his time "in service" (not on some type of radio call) he fills in his time by performing a number of valuable services . . . and driving around the streets alert for things which could jeopardize public safety. . . . But the fact remains that he essentially waits for offenders to commit their offenses, for these acts to be discovered and reported, and for himself to be assigned by radio to investigate these acts or to search for the offenders.[7]

POLICE AND THE PREVENTION PROGRAM

The organization of a prevention program is complex, but it consists of six basic steps: preliminary survey of prevention problems; authority for

[7]Charles P. McDowell, "The Police as Victims of Their Own Misconceptions," *The Journal of Criminal Law, Criminology & Police Science,* Vol. 62. No. 3 (1971), 435.

the program; determination of policy; relation of prevention to other community agencies; relation to departmental structure; and public relations.

The *preliminary survey* establishes the number, severity, age, and sex of the immediate delinquency problems and simultaneously clarifies community needs and the degree of police involvement. Regardless of how a prevention program is established, *authority* for the program must be clearly specified. This procedure "has been found imperative in order to avoid misunderstandings and malpractices by all concerned"[8] and can be initiated by the police chief, the department, or city or state ordinance. *Determination of policy,* based partially on the preliminary survey, is a vital step in focusing on the problem of prevention. At this level, the role and function of the juvenile specialist can be defined and integrated with the work of other police personnel. *Relation of prevention to other community agencies* has many ramifications but, in general, it clarifies the relation between police and other agencies and reduces the chance of redundance or excessive overlap in their efforts. In many instances, this step has proved of great value during another important point in prevention—evaluation of the program. Further advantages to evaluation and clarification will be discussed in later chapters.

With regard to *department structure,* relegated status for any segment of police work will reduce the chances for overall success. If delinquency prevention is not emphasized throughout the department, there is an implicit danger that all responsibility in this area will be relegated to the specialist. Recalling the earlier observation that police operations tend to focus on apprehension, departmental emphasis on joint responsibility for prevention is vital.

Public relations is an obviously crucial aspect of prevention. A strong public relations staff will be involved with delinquent and nondelinquent juveniles, the community at large, and other juvenile officers. It will be the liaison that communicates community opinion to the police, police philosophy to the community. Public relations will be more effective in some neighborhoods than others, but will also conceive of ways to increase communications and respect between the police and generally unsympathetic groups.

FROM POLICY TO PRACTICE

When the department acts on its policies, it is practicing *primary prevention*—that is, it takes direct and specific action to prevent delinquency in

---

[8]A. T. Brandstatter and J. J. Brennan, "Prevention Through the Police," in *Delinquency Prevention: Theory and Practice,* eds. W. E. Amos and C. T. Wellford (Englewood Cliffs, N.J.: Prentice-Hall, Inc., 1967), p. 201.

the community. Police involvement in PAL and other recreation programs is a form of primary prevention which translates public relations
policy into direct involvement.

Secondary prevention backs up primary prevention by identifying
problems and goals. The study of areas in which particular types of
delinquency seem to be fostered and the development of a prevention
program are examples of secondary prevention. Direct contact with the
community is not essential except at a fact-finding level.

The practices described in this section are, by definition, examples of
primary prevention. Effective prevention, however, requires both primary and secondary efforts. Experience in primary prevention is frequently of considerable help in developing secondary prevention programming.

Even in large departments with a great number of juvenile officers, the
patrol division probably has more direct contact with youth than any
other division. Contact between the patrol officer and the general public
is a considerable preventive force. (In the following, *delinquency* can of
course be substituted for *crime*.) "For a crime to take place, three factors
must exist simultaneously: (1) the *desire* . . . to commit the crime; (2) the
will . . . to commit the crime; (3) the *opportunity* . . . to commit the crime.
Should any of these factors be removed by the work of the patrol division,
the crime will not be successfully committed."[9]

When budget cuts reduce the patrol force, statistics indicate that crime
(including delinquency) increases. Of course, when the patrol officer is
on duty he is usually alert to catching juveniles in the process of committing a crime; he is seldom *conscious* of his role in crime prevention. But
the presence of police around the pool hall or favorite "hang-out" or the
knowledge that these areas are frequently patrolled obviously cuts down
even the desire for delinquency.

The ongoing programs geared specifically to juveniles are customarily
the work of the juvenile specialist. These police operations (sports, education, school liaison, and a host of similar activities) usually form the
basis of the primary prevention program by combining public relations
with concrete alternatives to delinquency. The juvenile officer's experience with and exposure to a neighborhood recreation program, for example, gives him a great deal of information about the community. This
knowledge can be extremely useful to secondary prevention planning.

Physical prevention—educating the public in methods of property security—is extremely effective secondary prevention. Meetings may be
organized in a home or office and the police will lecture on and demon-

[9]E. Eldefonso, A. Coffey, and R. Grace, *Principles of Law Enforcement* (New York: John
Wiley & Sons, Inc., 1968), p. 182.

strate the use of security devices to interested businessmen and home-owners in the community. Both large and small departments profit by assigning not only public relations specialists but detectives, patrolmen, and even administrative or executive staff to give these and similar demonstrations.

You have seen how primary and secondary prevention are carried out separately and cooperatively by public relations, patrol officers, juvenile specialists, community resources, and otherwise uninvolved citizens. It should be apparent that prevention effectiveness increases in proportion to the number of community and police elements involved.

Control

Whereas prevention and diversion try to involve the community, _control_ is almost exclusively a police procedure. When a delinquent has been neither prevented from committing an offense nor diverted from the justice system to rehabilitative community resources, he is subject to control. That is, the only alternative is to isolate him from the environment in which he has become delinquent in an effort to control further delinquency.

Control procedures, like prevention and diversion, are usually handled by all juvenile officers and are applied to a variety of offenses: shoplifting and other petty theft; car and bike theft and joy-riding; drug abuse; sexual delinquency; assaults; runaway juveniles; gang fights; school offenses such as extortion or vandalism; and adult involvement with juveniles and delinquents. (The neglected and abused child, also the responsibility of the police, will be discussed in the next chapter.)

Control involves the entire range of general police procedures, as well as those peculiar to juvenile cases: records, interviews, and interrogations; the rights of minors; arrest; court referrals; informers and entrapment; search and seizure; and intelligence networks, among others. Because procedure is central to this aspect of delinquency, control will be discussed in terms of the above categories.

RECORDS

The need for juvenile records is defensible on several grounds, but there is considerable controversy regarding the distinction between criminal records and juvenile records and the use of fingerprints and photographs in the latter. The controversial point is the confidentiality of juvenile records and subsequent use of fingerprint and photographic identification.

This issue is handled according to local discretion; there is no national standard. This method was given some approval in a report by the International Association of Chiefs of Police[10] and at least one advantage is the possibility for flexibility. Police procedure, to some extent, must conform to community feeling. Furthermore, local officers certainly have a better sense of which procedures apply to different juveniles. But general guidelines for record-keeping can prevent misuse of records and protect the rights of juveniles:

1. No juvenile fingerprints should be recorded in a criminal section of any essential fingerprint registry.
2. Because of the criminal connotations associated with fingerprints in the minds of many people, their use should be held to occasions where identification hinges upon evidence available only through their use and where sanctioned by law or juvenile court policies.
3. In many jurisdictions, the consent of the juvenile court must be obtained before such procedures are utilized.
4. Such fingerprints should be destroyed after the purpose has been served.[11]

The use of "mug-shots" and collection of data (beyond name, age, sex, and address) should be similarly limited. But police investigation obviously requires the collection of data, whether or not they are ultimately included in the records. Records themselves should be handled with great discretion and unnecessary information destroyed.

INTERVIEWS AND INTERROGATIONS

The ideal *interview* is conducted by one officer with one juvenile as a means of gathering general information incidental to an investigation. Formality is necessary only to the degree that the juvenile has a clear understanding of the officer's role. During an investigation, an officer may interview many juveniles—some suspected of an offense, some not.

An *interrogation* is also intended to gather information, but it involves the juvenile who has committed an offense, who has confessed to having committed an offense, or against whom there is considerable evidence of involvement in an offense.

[10]G. W. O'Connar and N. A. Watson, *Juvenile Delinquency and Youth Crime: The Police Role* (Washington, D.C.: The International Association of Chiefs of Police, 1964).

[11]E. Eldefonso, *Law Enforcement and the Youthful Offender* (New York: John Wiley & Sons, Inc., 1972), p. 279.

Both interviews and interrogations are meant to further a police investigation initiated by a complaint, an offense, questionable behavior, or family situation. Complete rapport may not be possible, but successful juvenile officers, because there is a great need to reduce emotional tension, conduct interviews and interrogations in a friendly and honest manner. They may open the talk with some general discussion of topics of interest to juveniles. This can be done without disguising the purpose of the talk or the need for cooperation and honesty.

Interviewing young children is often easier if their parents are present. In some cases this is not possible or is unwise, but when parents are available and are sincerely interested in their child's welfare, an investigation can be greatly facilitated by their presence. Requesting their presence is also an assurance that the police do not want to intimidate the child and are concerned with his overall welfare. If parental presence is disruptive or has a negative effect on the child, he can be reinterviewed alone. Except in rare cases, respect for authority is enhanced if the officer's manner is friendly and helpful. Courts reflect increasing concern for the child's rights and, aside from being unprofessional and otherwise undesirable, police behavior that hints of threat, insult, scorn, and other intimidating gestures or expressions is frequently interpreted as violation of rights.

Juvenile investigations tend to be quite complex. A child's memory, attention span, and emotions about the situation will color the information he gives. The officer conducting the interview or interrogation frequently finds it necessary to go over details repeatedly, to check and double-check facts—all the while attempting to make the child feel at ease so that he will not be additionally confused.

RIGHTS OF MINORS

On May 16, 1967, the United States Supreme Court, in *Gault* v. *Arizona,* handed down a landmark decision in juvenile cases. In 1964, the sheriff of Gila County, Arizona, took young Gerald Gault into custody following a neighbor's complaint about Gerald's alleged obscene phone calls. Neither of Gerald's parents was notified by the sheriff that their son had been taken into custody. It was almost by accident that they learned of a "hearing" to be held in the chambers of the juvenile court judge three days later.

At this hearing, no records were kept nor did the judge advise Gerald or his parents of his right to remain silent or the constitutional guarantee against self-incrimination. In the absence of records, later testimony from the judge and Gerald's mother was necessary. The judge testified that Gerald "confessed" to one of the indecent calls; Mrs. Gault swore that he confessed only to dialing the phone. In any event, an additional "hearing" was held three days later, at which time the Gault family's request to have the complaining party in court was denied by the judge. At this hearing the judge noted that, during the first hearing, Gerald had admitted making at least some of the indecent remarks alleged and committed him to a state correctional institution for six years—six years for a "crime," which, if committed by an adult, would have meant a maximum fifty-dollar fine. Commitment for this protracted period was based on the judge's finding that Gerald was a delinquent child (defined as "habitually involved in immoral matters"). The conclusion that he was "habitually" immoral appears to have been based on an *allegation* that Gerald was *reported* to have stolen another child's baseball glove two years earlier —a matter *not* brought before the juvenile court.

While most of the questions raised by the "procedures" of the Gault case relate more to juvenile court than the police, the Supreme Court response nevertheless impinges directly on police procedures. In effect, the Supreme Court declared that a juvenile has the right to: legal counsel; refusal to self-incriminate; confrontation of accusers and cross-examination; transcript of proceedings; and appellate review. These rights concern police procedure only when a child is in jeopardy of being arrested. Even then, only the first two (advisement of rights) are of major concern. Advisement typically follows this form:

Waiver of Rights and Warning

1. You have the right to remain silent and are not required to answer any questions.
2. Anything you say can and will be used against you in court.
3. You have the right to consult an attorney before you answer any questions, and an attorney may be present during the questioning.
4. If you have no funds to hire an attorney, the Public Defender will provide you with one to represent you at all stages of the proceedings.

When a child is being taken into custody, or is *likely* to be taken into custody, this advisement of rights is required. And the important consideration is that the child *understand* his rights. The level of language or example used should be whatever is appropriate to communicate this understanding to the child. *The significance of this procedure with juveniles is no less than with adults.*

ARREST

In general, an arrested person is, willingly or unwillingly, "in custody." In juvenile cases, however, the moment of arrest is not so clear. Some argue that, until he has been referred to juvenile court, a child has not been arrested; others believe that a child is "without freedom of movement" even when engaged in a conversation with the police and is therefore under temporary arrest. For the purpose of this discussion, a juvenile will be considered arrested at the point the police make clear to him that he is not free to leave.

The officer, then, must be certain the child understands: his rights; the officer's intention to arrest him; the cause of the arrest; and the officer's authority to make the arrest. Moreover, all the legal complexities of, among others, *probable cause, stop-and-frisk, warrants,* and *citizen arrests* apply to juvenile as well as adult arrests. Physical force leading to bodily injury is appropriate only when there is no other way to effect the arrest. Many jurisdictions require the use of handcuffs if the arrested adult has committed a felony. But, unless a juvenile poses a threat to his own or others' safety or property, this restraint is unnecessary and may reinforce the juvenile's image of himself as a "criminal."

Female juveniles are usually taken into custody in the presence of an adult female—a policewoman, female juvenile probation officer, or the girl's mother. This procedure decreases the possibility of sexual molestation charges against the arresting male officer.

JUVENILE COURT REFERRALS

If a juvenile is in temporary custody for an interview or being transported by a patrol unit to the juvenile bureau for the same purpose, there is clearly no need for court procedures. When a juvenile is placed in a *holding facility* or *detention home* for "further action," however, the further action ought to be the juvenile court. If court action is uncalled for, there are only a few justifications for detaining the child: no supervision; danger to himself; runaway; danger to public; or the need for investigation. Although the police have wide latitude in determining whether juvenile arrest is necessary, the ideal is the detention only of those who require court action or belong to one of the five categories above.

Referral to juvenile court is handled in different ways. In Pennsylvania and Tennessee, for example, *any* adult may file a juvenile court petition and thereby initiate court action. In California, only a probation officer, judge, or court clerk can file the juvenile court petition. The juvenile officer must refer a case to court according to the law in his state. Filing the petition means only that a written allegation of law violation by a minor has been filed. This process will be examined in more detail in a later chapter.

SEARCH AND SEIZURE

The rules for search and seizure of adults and juveniles are identical and derived from the Fourth Amendment of the Constitution: "The right of the people to be secure in their persons ... against unreasonable searches and seizures, shall not be violated, and no warrants shall issue, but upon probable cause, supported by oath or affirmation and particularly describing the place to be searched, and the persons or things to be seized. ..."

All of the sensitivity called for when informing the juvenile of his rights to silence and counsel must be applied to the procedures of search and seizure. In *Frank* v. *Maryland,* the Supreme Court established the right to *resist* unauthorized entry. The Constitution and the Supreme Court define individual rights in this area very clearly.

INFORMERS and ENTRAPMENT

In the course of interviews and interrogations, juveniles can be regarded as at least potential informers because of the information they may supply about others. But certain abuses of this potential deserve mention: "Many judges would not consider a juvenile informer as a reliable witness. From a mental health point of view, it is unfair to subject anyone, especially a juvenile, to the high risk of physical danger, emotional stress, and mental breakdown involved in being an informer."[12] The informer is stigmatized by both adults and juveniles. "Tattling" is usually discouraged in even the youngest child, and, in most circumstances, adolescents especially feel tremendous psychological pressure if they "cop out" on their peers, even out of fear for their own situation.

In addition to the risk of alienating a juvenile from his subculture, there is increasing public feeling against procedures which encourage informers and evidence obtained in this manner.

> While the search for satisfactory definitions as well as explanations of delinquency continues, the community faced with a social problem makes what provisions it can to protect and deal with the troublesome child and his family. The major responsibility in this task, as the community's frontline defense against crime and delinquency, has been assigned to the police and the juvenile court.[13]

Assuming this responsibility and simultaneously maintaining secondary prevention efforts, the police must avoid procedures that suggest exploitation of the juvenile. This approach obviously applies to entrapment—"the act of [police] inducing a person to commit a crime not

---

[12]National Council on Crime and Delinquency, "The Use of Juveniles as Informers in Drug-Abuse Matters: A Policy Statement," *Crime and Delinquency,* Vol. 18, No. 2 (1972), 130.

[13]S. M. Robinson, *Juvenile Delinquency: Its Nature and Control* (New York: Holt, Rinehart and Winston, Inc., 1963), p. 207.

contemplated by him, for [purposes] of [prosecuting] him."[14] No police procedure that induces a juvenile to commit an illegal act, whether or not there is an intent to prosecute, will be regarded sympathetically.

INTELLIGENCE NETWORKS

Although juvenile officers who check the pool halls and drive-in restaurants and maintain contact with school officials rarely consider the resulting feedback as an intelligence network, such information is often the informal basis of a portion of the police intelligence system.

Within what might technically be called a sensor matrix, juvenile officers are customarily sensitive to signs of: impending violence; drug abuse; impending (and past) law violation; gang (not group) activities; predelinquent behavior; adults contributing to delinquency; and such family problems as runaways, neglect, or abuse. Gathering this intelligence is frequently routine public relations work, but the effective juvenile officer maintains numerous contacts with individuals, organizations, and groups from whom he can learn extremely useful information in day-to-day casual conversation.

Summary

This chapter, which deals with the police role in diversion, prevention, and control, opened with an explanation of the importance of the law enforcement subsystem. But the need for cooperation between juvenile and other police officers was also stressed.

Prevention was presented as a broad-based social program in which police can play a limited but key role. Primary and secondary prevention were defined, and a variety of programs were explained in terms of these two programs.

Diversion was defined as the (primarily) police effort to turn the predelinquent away from further exposure to the delinquent subculture and involvement with juvenile justice. The philosophical basis for diversion was contrasted with the general public's attitude that diversion allows delinquents to remain in the community and continue to commit offenses. Examples of programs which offer alternatives to delinquency were cited.

Control of delinquency was explained in terms of the procedures used when both diversion and prevention have failed. Discussion of the procedures, a few of their controversial aspects, and juvenile rights provided the frame of reference for understanding the initial steps in delinquency control.

[14]*Black's Law Dictionary*, rev. 4th ed. (St. Paul, Minn.: West Publishing Co., 1968).

Questions

1. Do you think the predelinquent stands to gain more from diversion programs or control procedures? Explain your answer.
2. Do you think diversion methods may be more successful with some predelinquents than others? If you agree, hypothesize about which types of individuals might respond positively and which negatively. If you disagree, explain why diversion is helpful for all predelinquents.
3. Explain how the police role in prevention is limited. List some ways in which you think the community could cooperate in the prevention of delinquency.
4. Do you think that police in patrol cars are more or less efficient than one or two officers patrolling a neighborhood on foot? Explain. Which method do you think is more effective? Why?
5. Explain the Supreme Court decision that the *Gault* case was a violation of the rights of a minor.
6. Do you think police should expect juveniles to act as informers? Explain your answer.
7. In your opinion, what are the legitimate reasons for putting a juvenile in detention?
8. Describe the main points a police officer should remember when arresting a juvenile.
9. Why is there opposition to including fingerprints and photographs in juvenile records? Explain why you agree or disagree with the opposition.

Annotated References

AMOS, W. E., and C. T. WELLFORD, eds., *Delinquency Prevention: Theory and Practice.* Englewood Cliffs, N.J.: Prentice-Hall Inc., 1967. An excellent collection of writings on police and community involvement in effective delinquency prevention.

COFFEY, A., E. ELDEFONSO, and W. HARTINGER, *Human Relations: Law Enforcement in a Changing Community.* Englewood Cliffs, N.J.: Prentice-Hall, Inc., 1971. Broad coverage of the complexities of contemporary police public relations.

_____, *Police–Community Relations.* Englewood Cliffs, N.J.: Prentice-Hall, Inc., 1971. More compact discussion of issues covered in previous reference.

ELDEFONSO, E., *Law Enforcement and the Youthful Offender.* New York: John Wiley & Sons, Inc., 1972. Excellent elaboration of many of the technical procedures introduced in this chapter.

FLAMMANG, C. J., *Police Juvenile Enforcement.* Springfield, Ill.: Charles C Thomas, Publisher, 1972. Pragmatic explanation of procedural matters.

HAMANN, A. D., "Factors to Consider When Handling Young Offenders," *Police Work.* Milwaukee, Wis.: Milwaukee Technical College, Dec. 1968. The author's experience and expertise enhance his emphasis on the manner in which police perceive their role.

JEFFREY, C. R., *Crime Prevention Through Environmental Design.* Beverly Hills, Calif.: Sage Publications, Inc., 1971. An interesting examination of the designed environment and delinquency prevention.

KENNEY, J. P., and D. G. PURSUIT, *Police Work with Juveniles and the Administration of Juvenile Justice.* Springfield, Ill.: Charles C Thomas, Publisher, 1972. The fourth edition of this work remains an excellent sourcebook of readings in delinquency control.

KVARACEUS, W. C., "Delinquency Prevention: Legislation, Financing and Law Enforcement Are Not Enough," *National Council on Crime and Delinquency,* Vol. 15, No. 4 (1969).

MARTIN, J. M., "Toward a Political Definition of Juvenile Delinquency." Washington, D.C.: U.S. Dept. of Health, Education and Welfare, 1970. Background information on the Youth Service Bureau.

O'CONNAR, G. W., and N. A. WATSON, *Juvenile Delinquency and Youth Crime: The Police Role.* Washington, D.C.: International Association of Chiefs of Police, 1964. Good coverage of police attitudes and discretion in juvenile matters.

PLATT, A. M., "Saving and Controlling Delinquent Youth: A Critique," *Issues in Criminology,* Vol. 5, No. 1 (1970). Good critical elaboration of the rationale for treating juvenile offenders with compassion and concern.

RECTOR, M. G., "Statement Before the U.S. Senate Subcommittee to Investigate Juvenile Delinquency," *Crime and Delinquency,* Vol. 16, No. 1 (1970). Indepth investigation of the gap between public beliefs and delinquency realities.

ROBINSON, S. M., *Juvenile Delinquency: Its Nature and Control.* New York: Holt, Rinehart and Winston, Inc., 1963. Overall examination of the police and court role in delinquency control.

TOBIAS, J. J., and C. LACY, "A Guidance Oriented Police Youth Bureau," *Law and Order,* Vol. 18, No. 8 (1970). The police role in the Youth Service Bureau.

UNITED STATES DEPARTMENT OF HEALTH, EDUCATION AND WELFARE, *Police Services for Juveniles.* Washington, D.C.: U.S. Gov't. Printing Office, 1964.

WATSON, N. A., and R. N. WALKER, *Training Police to Work with Juveniles.* Washington, D.C.: International Association of Chiefs of Police, 1965. Elaboration of the role of the juvenile specialist.

WEINER, N. L., And C. V. WILLIE, "Decisions by Juvenile Officers," *American Journal of Sociology,* Vol. 77, No. 2 (1971). Discussion of the discretion involved in police-youth contact and diversion.

WINTERS, J. E., "The Role of Police in Prevention and Control of Delinquency," *Federal Probation,* Vol. 21, No. 2 (1957).

6

The Neglected or Abused Child

One of the most dramatic and certainly one of the most complex aspects of juvenile justice is the neglected or abused child. Police work in this area involves parents or guardians who, by virtue of police involvement, are considered potentially unfit. The adult police officer and the adult parent generally agree that the delinquent child is in need of straightening out. If nothing else, the adults can agree that the delinquent is a "bad kid." But what happens when the police are not questioning the child's behavior but the adult's? What happens when the evidence is against the parents instead of the child? In short, what happens when the crime is not *by* the child, but *against* the child?

Police involvement with neglected and abused children is almost invariably perceived as hostile to the parents rather than protective of the child. In this context, the police role is confusing and unrewarding, compounded by sometimes shocking evidence of the unbelievable abuse inflicted by some parents on their children.

PROTECTIVE DIVERSION

The neglected or abused child has a great deal in common with the predelinquent. For one thing, neither stands to gain from exposure to the rehabilitative measures commonly used with delinquents. Police efforts to divert both cases from that area of juvenile justice are most appropriate. Unlike the predelinquent, however, the neglected or abused child frequently is diverted to a different area of juvenile justice. The neglected or abused child shares with the predelinquent the potential for delinquency as a result of inadequate parental supervision. For this reason, too, there is a real disadvantage in introducing the neglected child to examples of destructive behavior patterns.

But diverting these cases frequently proves to be extremely difficult. To whatever degree the parents cooperate in remedying the problem, there is the implicit concession that a problem exists. *But even when no prosecution is forthcoming, the stigma attached to neglecting or abusing children is such that parental admission of a problem is extremely rare.*

In many instances, parental "cooperation" is obtained only because the juvenile court has the power of enforcement. If parents do not cooperate to the degree that there is no change in the child's situation, the parents can be prosecuted. Most jurisdictions empower the juvenile or family court and juvenile probation (or specially empowered social workers) to deal with the cases of neglected or abused children in what amounts to a separate juvenile justice system. Such an arrangement permits police to divert these matters away from the delinquent segment of juvenile justice and, at the same time, retain the legal authority so often necessary even in cases that have no adult prosecution pending.

Such an arrangement also emphasizes the child's well-being rather than the parent's possible prosecution. In other words, this approach eliminates the tragic situations that can occur when a remedy for the neglected or abused children depends on the criminal court conviction of their parent. And in jurisdictions that allow consideration of evidence that the child *is* neglected or abused, even if it cannot be specifically proved that the parents are responsible, police have more alternatives for coping with these tragedies.

Perhaps the significance of police action and intervention in many of these matters will emerge in the following discussion of, first, neglect and then abuse.

Child Neglect

The aversion of many police officers to neglected child cases is unfortunate but understandable. Although many investigations of reported neglect frequently reveal simple differences in standards for adequate care, cases of actual neglect are uncovered too often to merit discontinuation of police involvement. But any report of child neglect is difficult to handle, awkward to investigate, and the police tend to welcome "assistance" from well-meaning neighbors, relatives, or social workers.

The police commonly issue an informal warning to parents about the consequences of continued misconduct. In most cases, these warnings suffice—particularly when embellished with the officer's personal recall of tragedies involving lost or abandoned children. The general success of these warnings no doubt relates to the impression made by the presence and manner of the police officer.

INADEQUATE SUPERVISION AND THE UNFIT HOME

Either of these conditions is an obvious indication of neglect. Either or both may or may not figure in cases of child abuse. Determinations of adequacy and fitness are, in any case, difficult. Even within one home, the parents may have different standards for their children, and on any city block one can find as many examples of the "proper" method of child-raising as there are families.

> The laws relating to neglect of children vary widely from state to state, some outlining specific definitions of neglect and others defining the term very broadly or leaving definition to administrative discretion. The laws of New York State are somewhat typical of those that define neglect in specific terms. They apply to children under 16 whose parents or guardians fail to provide them with the physical necessaries of life, needed medical attention, and educational opportunities . . . to abandoned children, to those under unlawful or improper supervision in an illegal place, or to a child in such need of care or control "as to injure or endanger himself or others." Mental incapacity of a parent, together with cruelty, immorality, or depravity, are specific reasons for considering parents unfit to care for their children. In addition, children who are left in someone's care by their parents without being visited by them or without payments for their support for a year may be considered abandoned . . . and . . . in need of the state's protection.[1]

The unfit home may be unfit because it is filthy. But where does one draw the line between dirt and filth? How much filth is unhealthy? The five-year-old obviously needs more supervision than the twelve-year-old. But who is more neglected—the exceptionally responsible five-year-old or the careless, immature twelve-year-old?

[1] *Protective Service for the Children of New York City: A Plan of Action* (New York: Laurin Hyde Associates, 1962), p. 34.

Child Abuse

While much of what has been previously stated applies to both the neglected and abused child, child abuse indicates special circumstances and considerations which should be dealt with separately.

> Serious physical abuse of children is a phenomenon difficult to understand when we consider that our society is enjoying unprecedented prosperity . . . and an enlightened approach to mental health. . . . This society is at the same time emphasizing children's rights and parental responsibility in the development of well-adjusted personality . . . Yet, in the midst of all this progress, we in child welfare are witnessing a growing paradox. . . . Two brief situations will serve to illustrate some of the types and kinds of injuries inflicted on children.
>
> A five-year-old girl wandered innocently out onto a porch after being instructed not to do so. She was kicked back into the house, thrown across a room, and hit about the head and face with a frying skillet.
>
> A nine-month-old boy had his eye blackened, his fingers, face, and neck burned.[2]

Unfortunately, the implications here extend even beyond the individual. As the above material suggests, cases of child abuse are increasing, and although there is a corresponding increase in attention to the problem, this is an area of juvenile justice for which an answer to "why" seems terribly necessary.

With or without massive public attention, the police bear the responsibility for protecting the child and prosecuting his parents. And because juvenile court convictions require the same "beyond reasonable doubt" evidence as criminal court cases, investigation of abuse cases, always difficult, requires a great deal of careful work and observation.

THE BATTERED CHILD

Neglected children can be mistreated in many ways that are scarcely, if at all, visible to the untrained eye. Physical abuse is usually visible; in the case of the abused (or, more commonly, *battered*) child this is especially true, because the parents of such children typically do not beat them just once but fairly consistently. Any child displaying frequent "accidental" bruises, burns, and so on should be regarded as a possible victim of the *battered child syndrome.* The following example illustrates some of the problems involved in investigation of these cases.

[2]E. J. Merill, "Physical Abuse of Children—An Agency Study," *Protecting the Battered Child* (Denver, Colo.: The American Humane Association, 1962), p. 1.

Following reports of child abuse, a juvenile officer began an investigation of a mother who had literally sandpapered her three small daughters' buttocks until they were raw and then poured acid on the area. When the children cried, their heads were shaved. Reports of abuse were not considered "relevant" by the social worker whose caseload included the parents. Working with the probation officer, the police officer obtained x-rays of each child's arms. They revealed the numerous "healed breaks" typical of the battered child and caused by continual and violent jerking.

Although the children's mother, on advice of legal counsel, denied responsibility for the acid, head shaving, and previously broken arms, the probation officer was able to prepare a successful court case on the basis of inadequate parental supervision (there was no denying the children's injuries, which would not have happened had they been "adequately supervised").

The juvenile officer, continuing his investigation, found further evidence of the battered child syndrome. The mother had taken her daughters to different physicians each time a new injury was inflicted. This of course increased the likelihood that each new doctor would believe her story that the injury was an accident. This behavior is a generally reliable indication of the battered child syndrome.

Although the juvenile officer was advised by the district attorney that there was insufficient evidence for a conviction, evidence of coincidental "physician switching" and new injuries meant that the parents were given a forceful warning. And with the establishment of juvenile court jurisdiction over the children, the parents cooperated in a court-suggested plan for psychiatric treatment.

SEXUAL ABUSE

These cases, relatively few of which are pursued to the point of becoming official cases, are probably the most difficult for law enforcement to pursue and prosecute. Most sexual abuse is committed by a family member, and the shame of incest in this and most societies is such that the child's family often prefers to keep the crime private. That is, the police and other agencies are rarely called. The scope of this problem, therefore, is practically impossible to estimate.

"The child victim of sex crimes committed by adults is also the victim of neglect by the community. He is a forgotten child—a child whose presence, whose condition, and whose cry for help is unrecognized or ignored."[3] Children in this situation are doubly jeopardized. Raised to

[3]V. DeFrancis, *Protecting the Child Victim of Sex Crimes* (Denver, Colo.: The American Humane Association, 1965), p. 1.

"respect their elders," many of them simply never question the actions of a close relative, let alone a parent. If they do, they may receive some sympathetic understanding but little concrete help from another relative. The "incident" will be hushed up; the child will feel that he is a part of the whole shameful business and may assume that he also shares the blame and guilt. There is little possibility that he will feel certain enough of his role as victim to take his complaint outside the family.

When instances of sexual abuse of a child are brought to the attention of a social agency, it, too, will confront obstacles. The skills necessary to deal with the problem are highly sophisticated and relatively uncommon. They are only slightly more apt to be found in the personnel of a social welfare staff than in the general population. Furthermore, "the task of the agency is to keep the family together, if possible. If a child remains in the home and is severely attacked while the family is being served, the agency is criticized for not removing the child."[4]

And, for the police, the problem is at least as complex. Judgments regarding the need for court action are made more difficult by the conflicting influences of numerous authorities—social workers, psychiatrists, psychologists, clergymen, and relatives—all of whom have some degree of interest in helping the juvenile officer come to the "right" decision. And, bearing in mind the difficulty the child may have had in drawing attention to his problem, the law enforcement obligation, although clear, is difficult to execute. "Laws for reporting child abuse cases do not, of themselves, achieve protection of children. They constitute only a beginning—a first step in the process of marshalling community services on behalf of the abused child."[5]

The Law and Social Welfare

Police departments have been known to demonstrate some reluctance in collaborating with social service agencies—even those oriented toward protective services—in dealing with cases of child neglect and abuse. Similarly, the social worker may be disinclined to involve legal authorities in what appears to be a social problem.

The practical problem, of course, is the different orientation of these two community services. While both are concerned with the child's welfare, the police officer is required to deal with the problem in terms of possible law violation and the social worker thinks in terms of counseling

[4]S. Chaneles and D. Brieland, *Sexual Abuse of Children: Implications for Casework* (Denver, Colo.: The American Humane Association, 1967), p. 24.

[5]V. DeFrancis, *Marshalling Community Services—On Behalf of the Abused Child* (Denver, Colo.: The American Humane Association, 1966), preface.

and guidance. The "law" may interfere with "reeducation" and vice versa, although this by no means suggests that the individual juvenile officer does not wish to see the unfit home improved or that the social worker takes no interest in the law.

When each agency is willing to take into consideration the limitations, demands, and orientations of the other, the two can not only work together but complement each other in a manner that is especially beneficial to the child. For example, the social worker's criteria for judging homes unfit or children neglected can be very useful to the juvenile officer. When an officer is attempting to make distinctions, the social worker may have information on neighborhood standards that can help him determine whether a specific environment is absolutely or relatively unfit.

The social worker, too, probably maintains close relations with the public health nurse and similar community resources. These people can provide additional knowledge to help the officer determine whether, in fact, there has been a law violation.

Conversely, law enforcement can help social service agencies when there is indication that the child should be removed from the home. But when enforcement of this need is carried out by the agency, juvenile officers may feel that their role has been ignored and that, hence, the social services are skeptical of their abilities.

> The protective agency has a mandate to provide service when needed and an obligation to explore, study, and evaluate the facts of neglect and their effect on children. The agency carries responsibility for maintaining service until the conditions are treated and neglect is reduced. It has the additional obligation to invoke the authority of the juvenile court (or family court) when such action is deemed necessary to secure protection, care, and treatment of children whose parents are unable or unwilling to use the help offered by the agency.[6]

Social workers can be effective enforcement officers, although even the best trained may find the enforcement role difficult. But from the point of view of the juvenile justice *system,* the most appropriate approach to enforcement lies with the police. When the enforcement aspect of juvenile problems is transferred to another agency, the juvenile justice system as a whole loses cohesion, efficiency, and effectiveness.

Police attitudes toward their role in neglect and abuse cases also may complicate relations with social welfare agencies. "People just can't believe that some parents treat children callously . . . and are shocked and angry when confronted with the mounting evidence. Public indignation . . . is largely translated into punitive action against parents who trans-

---

[6]*Child Protective Services, 1967* (Denver, Colo.: The American Humane Association, 1967), p. 2.

gress our cherished ideals about family responsibility for children."[7] The police, involved in these cases in spite of strong personal feeling, may share this attitude rather than the less punitive outlook of protective agencies.

ALTERNATIVES AND REFERRALS

The juvenile probation officer is a frequent intermediary alternative between the police and the social worker. In jurisdictions where police do not have or do not want a part in screening neglect cases, the probation officer generally has the authority to do so. In fact, many jurisdictions involve the probation department directly with protective services because the probation officer is: a peace officer; an officer of the juvenile court; educated and trained to work with families; and responsible for the child's welfare. Many juvenile court judges, therefore, prefer the probation staff to handle as much of the processing of neglect and abuse cases as the jurisdiction allows.

The juvenile officer, then, can clarify and simplify his own responsibilities in these cases if he can involve others and use their specialized training and knowledge. Furthermore, opportunities for constructive change are increased when the juvenile officer is aware of the services and alternatives offered by other agencies and other approaches.

Finally, any evidence that a report or complaint has some validity, regardless of the form of neglect or abuse, requires a referral decision. There are four alternatives at this point:

1. Social agency referrals are useful when there is only minimal evidence or evidence indicates minimal severity or danger to the child; the protective service agency is most useful.
2. Juvenile probation referrals are helpful when evidence is minimal but the severity of the apparent neglect or abuse is maximal. These referrals draw on the resources of juvenile officers who are officers of the court trained in family counseling.
3. Juvenile court referrals are made when there is sufficient evidence and the child's welfare is in jeopardy.
4. Criminal court referrals (usually made through the district attorney) are made when the child's welfare remains in doubt even after juvenile court proceedings.

It is clear, then, that probation officers, judges, and prosecutors need not be involved with family problems that are the result of an occasional

[7]V. DeFrancis, *Review of Legislation: To Protect the Battered Child, A Study of Laws Enacted in 1963* (Denver, Colo.: The American Humane Association, 1966), p. 1.

outburst of temper. On the other hand, a social worker need not feel the responsibility for enforcement, prosecution, adjudication, and correction when it is clear that the child's welfare is threatened. The alternatives for referral maximize the capabilities and responsibilities and minimize the limitations of four rehabilitative procedures. The neglected or abused child and his family deserve every chance to stay together. But the child's present and future welfare is the primary concern.

Summary

Noting the difficulties inherent in dealing with "unfit" parents and comparing them to parents of the delinquent, we discussed the role of the police in terms of protective diversion. Neglected and abused children must be diverted from difficult home situations, if necessary, and from contact with delinquents in the juvenile justice system.

Neglect cases, which frequently involve subtle distinctions and judgments, may be facilitated if police collaborate with social service agencies. Battered children and juvenile victims of sexual abuse also may benefit if police collaborate with another agency. But, because there is a stronger chance of adult criminality in these cases, the probation officer, with his varied roles and connections, is the preferred choice.

Following a discussion of the advantage to both police and social agencies, the chapter concluded with a list of four increasingly authoritarian referral alternatives and described the situations in which each can be most beneficially applied.

Questions

1. What are some reasons for handling neglect and abuse cases and predelinquents in a similar fashion?
2. Compare the orientations of the police officer and the social worker.
3. Explain how collaboration with the social worker can be helpful to the police officer involved in a neglect case.
4. At what point do you think parental supervision is inadequate enough to require police attention? Define your own ideas of adequate parental supervision for juveniles between the ages of: infancy to four years; five to nine years; ten to thirteen years; fourteen to sixteen years; over sixteen.
5. Explain the difficulties involved in law enforcement investigation and prosecution of child abuse.
6. Describe police responsibility to the battered child.
7. Which of the three cases—neglect, battered child, or sexual abuse—do you think is most difficult for the police? Explain your answer.

Annotated References[8]

AMERICAN HUMANE ASSOCIATION, Denver, Colorado. A series of excellent pamphlets on nearly every aspect of neglect, abuse, and molestation; various authors (refer to footnotes 2–7 in this chapter for a few of these).

ELMER, E., "Hazards in Determining Child Abuse," *Child Welfare,* Vol. XLV, No. 1 (1966), 28–33. An excellent elaboration of the difficulties in assessing the extent of (particularly) sexual abuse.

FONTANA, V. J., *The Maltreated Child: The Maltreatment Syndrome in Children.* Springfield, Ill.: Charles C Thomas, Publisher, 1974. Outstanding elaboration of the battered child syndrome.

Protective Services for the Children of New York City: A Plan of Action. New York: Laurin Hyde Associates, 1962. A good example of the possible protective services for neglected or abused children.

UNITED STATES DEPARTMENT OF HEALTH, EDUCATION AND WELFARE, CHILDREN'S BUREAU, *The Child Abuse Reporting Laws: A Tabular View.* Washington, D.C.: U.S. Gov't. Printing Office, 1966. The narrative and statistical references provide dramatic corroboration of the frequency of child abuse.

[8]Note: The references of the preceding chapter also afford a context in which to consider the significance to the neglected and abused child of centralizing delinquency control, predelinquency, and police services.

7

Intake Investigation
and Court Reports

The processes involved in determining the need for and filing a juvenile court petition and preparing juvenile court cases and reports are critical. As I have pointed out previously, the decision to file a petition is the first step in labeling the juvenile. "While [protection of society] and action in the 'best interests' of children through 'individualized treatment' are worthy objectives, the adverse effect of this system on labeled delinquent youth is considerable."[1] Ideally, then, the police decision to take a minor into custody (or refer him further into the juvenile justice system even if not in custody) is made only when no alternatives are available and with full knowledge that labeling occurs as a consequence of seeking juvenile court action. (It must be emphasized that juvenile court action through petition is often found necessary in cases where the juvenile is *not* detained. For the purpose of clarifying the processes of petitioning, however, this discussion will be limited to juveniles in custody.)

[1]F. L. Faust, "Delinquency Labeling: Its Consequences and Implications," *Crime and Delinquency*, Vol. 19, No. 1 (1969), 46.

While the mechanics of filing the petition are of little consequence, the decision that court action is necessary is extremely significant. If either criminal or juvenile justice is to function as a system, the decision to seek court action following arrest is most appropriately made by the prosecutor, in the case of adult offenses, and by the juvenile probation officer in delinquency matters—both the prosecutor and the juvenile probation officer being responsible for presenting the case to the court. However, the police make the initial arrest and customarily play a key role in gathering much of the evidence on which the probation officer's decision is made.

Photo by Charles Tado, County of Santa Clara, California

The combined effort of police and probation officers (and also prosecutors in certain *contested* matters) in the process by which a decision is made regarding the necessity of court action and by which the subsequent court case is developed is commonly known as the *intake investigation*. This process divides into three categories—*legal, social,* and *court reports*—which are the bases for this discussion.

Legal Aspects of the Intake Investigation

Following the *Gault* decision, virtually all jurisdictions legislated specific time restrictions for various police, probation, and juvenile court processes. In other words, such language as "without delay" is being replaced with exact limitations on how long a juvenile can be detained before and after a petition is filed, the setting of dates for court hearings, and even the allowable time for court continuances. The "right to a speedy trial" is being given increased attention in juvenile courts throughout the land.

Accelerating the investigative pace of course strains both police and probation resources. But it also emphasizes the value of collaborative effort in approaching the delinquency problems of the community, and there are any number of legal points on which collaboration is required.

ADMISSIONS AND CONFESSIONS

At about the same time as the Supreme Court rulings in the Gault and Kent matters, another significant decision was handed down in the Miranda case.[2] The high court held that when police deprive anyone of their freedom of movement in any manner, they must also advise the detained person of his rights and warn him against self-incrimination:

1. You have the right to remain silent.
2. Anything you say will be used against you.
3. You have the right to an attorney's presence.
4. An attorney will be provided if you cannot afford one.

While the Miranda case was an adult criminal matter, the combination of high court decisions in *Kent, Miranda,* and *Gault* left little doubt that the same constitutional rights applied to juveniles from whom police might obtain admissions or confessions.

> During a raid upon a suspected center for heroin sales, narcotics agents determine that one of the suspects taken into custody is a seventeen-year-old male. Juvenile officers are summoned and a decision is made to place the boy in juvenile hall.
>
> Although there is no biochemical evidence of "use" and no criminalistic evidence of "possession," the juvenile is nonetheless charged with "pushing" (selling) and "using" instead of being simply charged with violation of laws that prohibit "being in a place where narcotics or dangerous drugs are used or sold." The stronger charge is based upon an admission made by the juvenile to the arresting officers.
>
> The juvenile probation officer is given a police report that records the "advisement of rights" prior to the admission. A decision is made to file a petition, continue detention, and prepare a court case. Subsequent police and probation investigation determines that the juvenile is living alone without parental control and *may be* involved in an elaborate drug-sales network on several high school campuses.

[2]*Miranda* v. *Arizona,* 384 U.S. 436 (1966).

Again, after the juvenile is advised by the probation officer of his rights, he admits involvement in the "narco-ring," adding that he is unconcerned with juvenile court wardship.

Waiver of Juvenile Court Jurisdiction

As in most states, the probation officer was aware of statutory latitude to recommend to the juvenile court that the minor be found "an unfit subject," meaning that age, sophistication, nature of offense, lack of parental control (and, in many cases, prior record) seem to eliminate the likelihood that *juvenile* court would prove useful—adult court appearing more appropriate.

After such a recommendation was made in this case, the juvenile denied ever having admitted anything to anyone.

Given this set of circumstances, the police-probation intake investigation was a "success" in juvenile court to the extent that the probation officer's recommendation and police evidence persuaded the judge to *waive* juvenile court jurisdiction. As an overall intake investigation, however, it was a failure because the adult court dismissed the case for lack of *admissible* evidence (recall the absence of biochemical or criminalistic evidence).

The reason that the adult case was dismissed is in part due to the ruling by the United States Court of Appeals in the Harling matter.[3] This decision held that "to allow admissions made by the child in the noncriminal and nonpunitive setting of juvenile court procedures to be used later for the purposes of securing his criminal conviction and punishment" would offend many of the principles of justice.

As a practical matter, therefore, the petition should have alleged nothing more than could have been proven *without* an admission or confession—evidence that stands on its own merit—particularly if there appears to be any chance of one or a combination of the following: the matter will be referred to adult court; the admission will be withdrawn and denied; or part or all of the petition will be contested. Not surprisingly, the addition of (or changes in) attorneys frequently causes such changes in the overall process.

Had police-probation collaboration reduced either the charge or the petition allegation (or both) to the provable violation of the law that prohibits "being in a place where narcotics or dangerous drugs are sold or used," the criminal court prosecutor may have been able to move against the high school drug ring. Of course, physical evidence—in this case—was missing. In addition to chemical and biochemical evidence, the intake investigation also makes frequent use of such criminalistic evidence as fingerprints, voiceprints, graphology, ballistics, and specto-

[3] *Harling* v. *United States,* 295 F. 2nd 161 (1961).

graphic, serological, toxicological, metallurgical, and radiological anal-yses. The manner in which this evidence is obtained often must take into account the individual's constitutional rights.

SEARCH AND SEIZURE

Juvenile search and seizure rights, discussed in the previous chapter, obviously must be considered during the intake investigation. Indeed, evidence obtained in support of an allegation made in a juvenile court petition may be used only if it has been obtained with a search warrant or *probable cause.*[4] Furthermore, evidence obtained without a search warrant or probable cause cannot be used in determining if juvenile court action is called for.

Evidence obtained *with* a valid search warrant is admissible except in very rare cases. But probable cause is often difficult to prove or disprove. "Reasonable grounds to believe means 'a reasonable ground or suspicion supported by circumstances sufficiently strong in themselves to warrant a cautious man in believing the accused guilty.' The word 'suspicion' does not mean mere suspicion. Nor does *probable cause,* or as sometimes stated, 'reasonable cause to believe,' depend upon the outcome."[5] Evidence gathered on the basis of probable cause is often admissible, but police must have a clear idea of what is and what is not sufficiently probable cause.

A related matter is the preservation of evidence.

THE PRESERVATION OF EVIDENCE

Each police or probation officer who has had evidence in his personal possession between the time it was gathered and the time it is presented in court becomes a link in the chain regarding the validity of the evidence. For example:

> A juvenile probation officer takes into custody a court ward on probation whom he has been supervising, suspecting the juvenile of drug abuse. Various pills and a substance in a plastic bag are found on the person of the minor. This evidence is left by the probation officer on the desk of a police narcotics detective, with an attached note instructing the detective to have a crime lab analysis made.
>
> A juvenile police officer takes a group of juveniles into custody at an unsupervised party at which he located similar evidence. The juvenile officer also

---

[4]For clarification of the many facets of probable cause, see: 33 ALR 609 private person; 44 ALR 149 liquor; *State* v. *Pickens,* 160 So. 2nd 577 (LA 1974); *People* v. *Frank,* Cal. Rptr. 202 (Dist. Ct. Appeals, 1964); and *Irley* v. *U.S.,* 314 F. 2nd 251 (C.A.D.C. 1963).

[5]*State* v. *Cox,* 262 Wis. 303 (1952).

leaves the evidence with written instructions on the same narcotic detective's desk.

The narcotics detective emerges from his watch commander's office shortly after these two sets of evidence have been left, only to find several officers picking up both sets of evidence from the floor following an accident when two officers had attempted to answer the unattended telephone.

Although the notes from the juvenile probation officer and the juvenile police officer were detached during the accident, all officers involved in picking up the evidence are "pretty sure" each note has been returned to the proper evidence.

Nothing more is thought of the matter until laboratory analysis reveals that one of the sets is barbiturates, amphetamines, and marijuana and the other is reginold—a substance similar to marijuana—and harmless placebos used in psychological experiments.

The chain of evidence has been broken in so many ways that neither the probation officer nor the police officer can use it. Had either the probation officer or the police officer taken their evidence directly to the crime lab, the chain would not have been broken. Indeed, had the probation officer presented his evidence directly to the lab, only the testimony of the technician receiving the evidence and the probation officer would have been necessary to clearly establish that the evidence in court was the same evidence obtained originally. Common-sense procedures in such matters serve the intake investigation well.

WITNESSES AND LINE-UPS

A wide range of interviews are ordinarily necessary to complete an intake investigation—particularly if there are victims. Discussion of restitution for destroyed, stolen, or lost property, attitudes regarding the juvenile, and many other variables enhance the total understanding of the case. Witnesses may provide either circumstantial evidence or eye-witness testimony for a pending juvenile court hearing. Such interviews are a major portion of the intake investigation.

The Supreme Court has held that _due process_ invalidates line-up methods and procedures that are so "impermissively suggestive as to give rise to a very substantial likelihood of irresponsible misidentification.[6] Police and probation officers who use the line-up for identification of an accused minor are responsible for demonstrating that the line-up in no way influences the testimony of witnesses later appearing in juvenile court to identify the minor.[7]

[6] *Simmons* v. *United States,* 388 U.S. 293.
[7] D. R. Nedurd, *The Supreme Court and the Law of Criminal Identification* (Chicago: L. E. Publishers, 1969), p. 255.

The accused may remain silent without being penalized. But neither the Fifth nor Sixth Amendment prohibits the use of the line-up. Indeed, refusal to cooperate in such *nontestimonial* procedures may be cited in juvenile court by the probation officer without violating the rights guaranteed by either amendment. The difference between testifying against himself and participation in nontestimonial procedures should be made clear, however. The matters discussed here reflect most of the significant legal variables in the process of determining if juvenile court action is needed and, if needed, the legal foundations on which the court case will be developed. The gathering of social information, when combined with the legal data, forms the basis of the decision to either file a juvenile court petition or pursue other alternatives.

Social Aspects of the Intake Investigation

To some degree, the gathering of social information is more the task of the probation officer than the police officer. Once sufficient legal evidence has been developed to verify the allegations in a petition, it is the probation officer's responsibility to prepare a court report. The court report, like the rest of the intake investigation, has two parts: *legal* (jurisdictional) and *social* (dispositional).

Social information is gathered from interviews with the minor and his parents, teachers and counselors, clergymen, neighbors, victims, physicians, and any other individuals who have had meaningful contact with the minor.

Ideally, such interviews occur in the minor's home, neighborhood, and school and thus provide additional reality to the decision regarding a petition and recommendation for juvenile court disposition.

If there is sufficient legal information to document a law violation and if the social information also confirms the necessity for filing a petition, the petition is filed and the probation officer must prepare a report for the juvenile court.

Court Reports

If petitions are contested, the juvenile court hearing is likely to be *bifurcated* into a jurisdictional and a dispositional phase (this is explained in the following chapter). A similar division of the court report therefore seems appropriate. While there is no standard format among the hundreds of probation agencies preparing these reports, simply dividing the report into two parts is sensible and clear.

Part I. Jurisdiction

1. Petition:

Begin with, "The petition filed (*date*) by the probation officer alleges" for *each* petition filed.

2. Legal counsel:

"None" or name of attorney and whom he represents.

3. Reason for hearing:

Summary of probation and police investigation as it relates to the specific allegations of the petition or purpose of hearing.

4. Statement of witnesses/victim:

Include whether each has been subpoenaed.

5. Statement of minor:

State whether minor (or minor and parent in dependent cases) admits or denies the allegations of the petition.

6. Recommendations:

Follow format prescribed in standard probation officer's report recommendations.

Part II. Social Study

1. Previous referrals:

Refer to last court report for previous referrals and include any new referrals in the current report. Should there be obvious errors in last court report, probation officer will correct.

2. Present whereabouts of minor:

Tell where the minor can be reached. If he is not in custody, explain circumstances.

3. Additional circumstances:

Include additional law violations and indicate whether denied or admitted, other detrimental conditions in dependent cases, and relevant information regarding co-participants, restitution, injuries, property damage, referrals to other agencies, etc.

4. Adjustment under supervision

If the minor is currently under supervision, name the probation officer or social worker. Summarize minor's adjustment and family dynamics while under supervision and in placement.

5. Statement of minor:

Attitude toward overall present situation and future.

6. Statement of parents/guardian

Each parent whenever possible. Include their attitude toward the offense and any plan they may have.

7. Statement of relative or foster parents:

8. School report:

The name of the school the minor is attending or last attended is to be dictated in the first sentence. Include the minor's current adjustment as to attendance, grades, and behavior, and school plan for the minor.

9. Juvenile hall/shelter report:

10. Psychological, psychiatric, or medical reports:

Summarize. Include examination date and name of examining agency.

11. Personal and family background:

Include marital status of parents, who has legal custody of the minor, occupation of parents and source of family income, number and court status of siblings, unusual health problems of family members (if significant), summary of arrest record of parents, and other significant information, such as condition of housing.

12. Evaluation:

Indicate dynamics of minor's and/or family's behavior and reasons for recommendations.

13. Dispositional recommendations:

Follow format prescribed in standard probation officer's report recommendations.

One of the most significant sections in the above format is *Evaluation.* In this section of the report, the probation officer can provide the court with a *rationale* for the recommendation. An evaluation of both the jurisdictional and the dispositional phases may also assist the court in assessing the relationship between the minor's rights and needs.

In jurisdictions that provide full copies of the court report to defense counsel, the combined evaluation and recommendation may serve to clarify for the juvenile:

1. Conflicting data or evidence gathered during the intake investigation.
2. Methods used to resolve such conflict.
3. Overall dimensions of the problem.
4. Apparent causal factors.
5. Plans for remedy of problems encountered (frequently of greatest interest).

Summary

This chapter introduced the collaborative efforts of police and probation officers as the basis for the intake investigation—the process by which the necessity for filing a juvenile court petition is determined and, if so, the process by which the court case is prepared.

Confessions, search and seizure, evidence preservation, victims, witnesses, and line-ups were discussed as elements of the *legal* segment of the intake investigation. The juvenile, his family and home, school, neighborhood, and community are areas of concern in the *social* portion.

The court report, which also reflects these two concerns, and the intake investigation itself correspond to the jurisdictional (legal) and dispositional (social) phases of the contested petition hearing.

A suggested format for the court report included a section for the probation officer's overall evaluation of the case. His evaluation also provides a rationale for the recommendation made to the court.

Questions

1. In terms of significance, contrast the mechanics of filing a petition to the *decision* to file a petition.

2. Discuss the significance of admissions and confessions during the intake investigation.

3. What is the purpose of the intake investigation?

4. Discuss search and seizure in terms of the intake investigation.

5. Explain the importance of preservation of evidence.

6. Do you think the social investigation is worthwhile? Explain your answer.

7. How might the information gathered from the social investigation be used to diagnose the juvenile's problem? Describe how the diagnosis might be used.

8. In what way can the probation officer's evaluation assist the defense attorney?

Annotated References

CICOUREL, A. V., *The Social Organization of Juvenile Justice.* New York: John Wiley & Sons, Inc., 1968. A good discussion of the collaborative efforts of police and probation and additional dimensions of the social aspects of the intake investigation.

ELDEFONSO, E., *Law Enforcement and the Youthful Offender.* New York: John Wiley & Sons, Inc., 1972. Excellent elaboration of the police role in the intake investigation.

EMERSON, R. M., *Judging Delinquents: Context and Process in Juvenile Court.* Chicago: Aldine-Atherton, Inc., 1969. Good general discussion of the evaluation section of the court report.

FOX, S. J., *The Law of Juvenile Courts in a Nutshell.* St. Paul, Minn.: West Publishing Co., 1971. Outstanding coverage of the judicial (legal) implications of the court report.

GARABEDIAN, P. G., and D. C. GIBBONS, *Becoming Delinquent: Young Offenders and the Correctional System.* Chicago: Aldine-Atherton, Inc., 1970. Good discussion of the juvenile court deposition removing minor from home.

KOHUT, N. C., *The Probation Officer Reports in Court.* Chicago: Family Law Research Publications, 1966. An excellent elaboration of one approach to the court report.

KRASNOW, E. G., "Social Investigation Reports in the Juvenile Court—Their Uses and Abuses," *Crime and Delinquency,* Vol. 12, No. 2 (1966). A singularly well-written examination of several dimensions of the social aspects of the intake investigation.

LOHMAN, J. D., J. T. CAREY, J. GOLDFARR, and M. J. ROWE, *The Handling of Juveniles from Offense to Disposition.* Berkeley, Calif.: University of California Press, 1965. Good development of the numerous ramifications of these processes.

McHARDY, L. W., "The Court, the Police, and the School," *Federal Probation,* Vol. 32, No. 1 (1968). Elaboration of the police role in certain social aspects of the intake investigation.

NEWMAN, G. G., ed., *Children in Courts: The Question of Representation.* Ann Arbor, Mich.: The Institute of Continuing Legal Education, 1967.

8

Rights Versus Needs

Having developed some acquaintance with the organization of juvenile justice and the procedures preliminary to court appearance, it is appropriate to examine the courtroom process itself. This process and the decision which results are largely defined by prevailing philosophies, themselves directly and indirectly determined by public opinion and high court decisions.

Probably the most remarkable feature of the contemporary juvenile court is its transition from concern with needs (*parens patriae*) toward concern for the juvenile's rights. In many ways, the current juvenile court is in between the clinically oriented juvenile courts of the past and the ultimately balanced court of the future.

Only a few astute observers (for example, Roscoe Pound, whose writings are cited throughout this volume) anticipated the inevitability and direction of this change, but national attention has been drawn to it by recent Supreme Court decisions, particularly the landmark *Gault* decision, described in Chapter 5. Inasmuch as it remains the most significant Supreme Court action relating to juvenile court, further elaboration of the Gault case is necessary to any understanding of the current juvenile court.

Photo by Charles Tado, County of Santa Clara, California

Juvenile Justice after Gault

Before elaboration of the impact of the *Gault* decision, a review of the basic situation may prove useful. On little more than a neighbor's allegation, Gerald Gault was taken into custody on suspicion of having made one or more lewd phone calls. His parents were not notified of his arrest; neither the juvenile nor his parents were advised of his right to counsel; the juvenile court *refused* to require a court appearance by his accuser; and no official court records were kept at the hearing. Of additional concern to the Supreme Court was the absence of clear notification of the pending juvenile court proceedings that were to incarcerate the child for many years.

In the majority opinion, ". . . unbridled discretion, however benevolently motivated, is frequently a poor substitute for principle and procedure. . . . We do not mean . . . to indicate that the hearing to be held must conform to all of the requirements of a criminal trial or even of the usual administrative hearings; but we do hold that the hearings must measure up to the essentials of due process and fair treatment."[1] But beyond this

[1]Supreme Court (No. 116, October Term, 1966), *In Re Gault,* 386 U.S. (May 15, 1967).

succinct opinion, the Supreme Court set in motion a virtual overhaul of
juvenile court procedure:

> *Gault,* however, commands a virtual overhaul of the juvenile court process
> both procedurally and geographically. For in that case, the Court found sev-
> eral main "arrest" and "trial" procedures, which were subscribed to by most
> juvenile court systems, constitutionally invalid.
>
> In particular the Court held that the defendant: (1) had to be notified in
> writing of the specific charges; (2) had to be told of his right to counsel,
> including his right to court-appointed counsel if he could not afford to retain
> counsel; (3) had to be told of his right not to testify; and (4) had the right to
> demand that complaining witnesses appear in court and be cross-examined.
> Heavily undermined, if not swept away entirely, was the fiction that juvenile
> processes were civil rather than criminal in nature and consequently not sub-
> ject to the commands which the fourteenth amendment's due process clause
> imposed upon criminal proceedings.[2]

At the time of the *Gault* decision, there were 2,671 juvenile courts in
the United States and Puerto Rico.[3] The structure and status of each
court within each jurisdiction varied then and now: some are separate,
independent courts, but most are a part of superior, county, municipal,
circuit, district, common pleas, or probate courts. In a few jurisdictions
family courts deal with domestic relations, delinquency, dependency, and
neglect. The number of juvenile courts has grown and the variation in
their structure and operation has continued in the years since the *Gault*
decision. The complexity of implementing changes suggested by the
Gault decision is, of course, dependent on the specific preexisting court
structure and philosophy. Fortunately, many court proceedings were already in compliance with standards set by the Supreme Court decision
on Gault.

BIFURCATION AND DUE PROCESS

Bifurcated means separated into two branches. A bifurcated proceeding
in juvenile court is one which separates the fact-finding and decision-
making functions of the court. The *Gault* decision stressed not only the
necessity of due process but also the importance of the bifurcated proceeding. The original local hearings in the Gault case were obviously a

[2]B. C. Canon, and K. Kolson, "Rural Compliance with Gault: Kentucky, A Case Study,"
Journal of Family Law, Vol. 10, No. 3 (1971), 301.

[3]The President's Commission on Law Enforcement and Administration of Justice, *Task
Force Report: Juvenile Delinquency and Youth Crime* (Washington, D.C.: U.S. Gov't.
Printing Office, 1967), p. 4.

violation of due process: Gerald Gault had not been advised of his rights. And there was no separation of the fact-finding and disposition functions of the hearing. But, until the Supreme Court decision in this matter, due process and bifurcation had not been guaranteed to the juvenile. The "informality" of the juvenile court had implied, in some jurisdictions, a certain procedural flexibility and liberality.

The *Gault* decision should have been no surprise to those capable of seeing the handwriting on the wall. A year earlier, in *Kent* v. *United States*,[4] the juvenile court of Washington, D.C. was found in error when it waived jurisdiction over a sixteen-year-old and released him to the adult court without granting him a juvenile court hearing on the waiver. Not only was he entitled to such a hearing, ruled the Supreme Court, but also to the procedural safeguards of due process in the course of the hearing.

The *Kent* and *Gault* decisions effectively redefined the nature of the juvenile court. No longer were its proceedings civil, for if the rights of juveniles and adults are the same in matters of the law, the procedures of juvenile and adult court are theoretically identical, also. Therefore, juvenile court is, in this sense, also a criminal court.

In 1970, *in re Winship*,[5] the Supreme Court further expanded the due process rights of the juvenile. Comparing the potential and equal threat to rights inherent in juvenile and criminal court proceedings, the Supreme Court found that a juvenile court petition must be proved true beyond reasonable doubt. The amount of evidence previously needed was only "a preponderance." The Supreme Court indicated, however, that the removal of the "civil evidence standard" was not to affect the informality, flexibility, or efficiency of the fact-finding hearing in a juvenile case.

JUVENILE JURIES

In the case of *McKeiver* v. *Pennsylvania*,[6] the Supreme Court held that a trial by jury is not constitutionally required in state proceedings. The Court denied that the jury is "a necessary component of accurate fact-finding," Justice Blackmun pointing out that juries are not used in probate court, deportation proceedings, nor military trials. If the jury was incorporated in juvenile court proceedings, the court foresaw the full-scale conversion of juvenile proceedings into criminal courts and the negation of the need for a separate system.

[4]*Kent* v. *United States*, 383 U.S. 541 (1966).
[5]*In re Winship*, 397 U.S. 358 (1970).
[6]*McKeiver* v. *Pennsylvania*, 403 U.S. 528 (1971).

The significance of the Supreme Court position is its emphasis on retaining a separate juvenile system, although there are at least eleven states in which juries are allowed in specific juvenile cases.[7]

Rights Then Needs

Another way to define the bifurcated juvenile court procedure is the distinction between a juvenile's rights and his needs. Juvenile rights (due process) are guaranteed him by the Constitution, as interpreted by the Supreme Court. His needs are summed up in the dissenting opinion of Justice Stewart in the *Gault* decision:

> Juvenile proceedings are not criminal trials. They are not civil trials. They are simply not adversary proceedings. Whether treating with a delinquent child, a neglected child, a defective child, or a dependent child, a juvenile proceeding's whole purpose and mission is the very opposite of the mission and purpose of a prosecution in a criminal court. The object of the one is correction of a condition. The object of the other is conviction and punishment for a criminal act.[8]

But needs and rights need not be conflicting concerns in juvenile court. If there is no proper guarantee of rights, there can be no guarantee that needs are being properly considered. Rights are of primary importance during the fact-finding process of juvenile court; when the judge considers the disposition of the case (being assured that his decision is based on proper application of due process), he has the opportunity to assess the juvenile's needs and act accordingly.

> In their zeal to care for children neither juvenile judges nor welfare workers can be permitted to violate the Constitution, especially the constitutional provisions as to due process that are involved in moving a child from its home. The indispensable elements of due process are: first, a tribunal with jurisdiction; second, notice of a hearing to the proper parties; and finally, a fair hearing. All three must be present if we are to treat the child as an individual human being and not to revert, in spite of good intentions, to the more primitive days when he was treated as a "chattel."[9]

A ward of the court might be a delinquent, a predelinquent, or a neglected or abused child. While the court's jurisdiction is essentially the

---

[7]N. L. Nathanson, "Jury Trial—Juvenile Court," *The Journal of Criminal Law, Criminology and Police Science,* Vol. 62, No. 4 (1971), 497–504.

[8]*In re Gault.*

[9]A. Lehman, "Juvenile's Right to Counsel in a Delinquency Hearing," 17 *Juvenile Court Judge's Journal* 53, 54 (1966).

same in each case, there is some value in distinguishing between delinquent and abused wards.

Most jurisdictions handle this distinction by declaring proof of neglect or abuse grounds for declaring the minor a *dependent child of the court.* The juvenile who has been proved guilty of delinquency is declared a *ward of the court.* In both cases, the proceedings are *on behalf of,* rather than *against,* the minor. However, because the main purpose of the distinction is to remove from the abused or neglected child all stigma of delinquency, the approach to agreeing on court jurisdiction ordinarily differs.

RIGHT TO CONTEST: ADVERSARY HEARING

Contested matters best illustrate the bifurcated juvenile court proceeding. Although the term *adversary* has a generally negative connotation, an adversary hearing is simply the juvenile's opportunity to contest the allegations against him—to insist that an "advocate," if desired, challenge the evidence being presented and request the court to weigh evidence of the juvenile's possible innocence against evidence of his possible guilt.

The applicability of due process and the procedure for adversary hearings were emphasized when the Supreme Court reacted to "the particular elements which constitute due process in a juvenile court hearing. . . . Neither man nor child can be allowed to stand condemned by methods which flout constitutional requirements of due process of law."[10]

NOTICE OF CHARGES AND PETITION

Being advised of the specific, alleged offenses or conditions brought against him is the right of every minor. Moreover, his parents or guardians also are entitled to specific knowledge of these allegations.

> Notice, to comply with due process requirements, must be given sufficiently in advance of scheduled court proceedings so that reasonable opportunity to prepare will be afforded, and it must "set forth the alleged misconduct with particularity." It is obvious . . . that no purpose of shielding the child from the public stigma of knowledge of his having been taken into custody and scheduled for hearing is served by [a deferred] procedure. . . . Even if there were a conceivable purpose served by the deferral . . . it would have to yield to the requirements that the child and his parents or guardian be notified, in writing, of the specific charge or factual allegations to be considered at the hearing, and that such written notice be given at the earliest practicable time, and in

[10] *In re Gault.*

any event sufficiently in advance of the hearing to permit preparation. Due process of law requires notice of the sort we have described—that notice which would be deemed constitutionally adequate in a civil or criminal proceeding. It does not allow a hearing to be held in which a youth's freedom and his parents' right to his custody are at stake without giving them timely notice, in advance of the hearing, of the specific issues that they must meet. Nor, in the circumstances of this case, can it reasonably be said that the requirement of notice was waived.[11]

Most jurisdictions require the filing of a petition "on behalf of the minor" which initiates juvenile court action and specifies the allegations. But the petition, or at least pertinent sections of it, can serve as a written notice of charges. Because even the hearing of juvenile court petitions in most instances implicitly threatens a juvenile's liberty, Supreme Court concern with due process in this and other juvenile court procedures is obviously justified.

RIGHT TO COUNSEL

Having considered the rights that arresting officers must specify to juveniles taken into custody (see Chapter 5), the comments of the Supreme Court on the right to counsel are probably sufficient here:

> We conclude that the Due Process Clause of the Fourteenth Amendment requires that in respect of proceedings to determine delinquency which may result in commitment to an institution in which the juvenile's freedom is curtailed, the child and his parent must be notified of the child's right to be represented by counsel retained by them, or if they are unable to afford counsel, that counsel will be appointed to represent the child.[12]

Perhaps this is the most significant factor—the clearly defined right of the minor to an advocate who can contest the allegations of the juvenile court petition, even though the petition was filed on the minor's behalf. This right may or may not be exercised, but it remains as much a right for the juvenile as the adult, as do the rights to confront one's accuser and to avoid self-incrimination.

CONFRONTATION, CROSS-EXAMINATION, AND SELF-INCRIMINATION

The right to face one's accuser is the clearest indication that the juvenile now has the right to contest allegations in an adversary manner. Being

[11] *In re Gault.*
[12] *In re Gault.*

able to cross-examine the accuser dramatizes the similarity of the *contested* juvenile court case and the adult criminal court case:

> Since the United States Supreme Court has held that to deprive an accused of the right to confront and cross-examine the witnesses against him is a denial of due process under the Fourteenth Amendment, the application of normal notions of due process to juveniles would invalidate the use at adjudication of all portions of the social report which are based upon hearsay evidence. Moreover, the Gault case makes it clear that such evidence cannot be the sole basis for a delinquency finding. It does not, however, directly hold that such evidence is generally inadmissible as is the case in other areas of the law.[13]

Less dramatic but no less significant is the right to remain silent, and the Supreme Court is no less eloquent on this constitutional safeguard:

> The privilege against self-incrimination is, of course, related to the question of safeguards necessary to assure that admissions or confessions are reasonably trustworthy, that they are not the mere fruits of fear or coercion, but are reliable expressions of the truth. The roots of the privilege are, however, far deeper. They tap the basic stream of religious and political principle because the privilege reflects the limits of the individual's attachment to the state and—in a philosophical sense—insists upon the equality of the individual and the state. In other words, the privilege has a broader and deeper thrust than the rule which prevents the use of confessions which are the product of coercion because coercion is thought to carry with it the danger of unreliability. One of its purposes is to prevent the state, whether by force or by psychological domination, from overcoming the mind and will of the person under investigation and depriving him of the freedom to decide whether to assist the state in securing his conviction.
>
> It would indeed be surprising if the privilege against self-incrimination were available to hardened criminals but not to children. The language of the Fifth Amendment, applicable to the states by operation of the Fourteenth Amendment, is unequivocal and without exception. And the scope of the privilege is comprehensive.[14]

The rights discussed thus far apply unequivocally to juveniles. In terms of the right to a transcript of proceedings and appellate review, however, a precise interpretation is more difficult.

RIGHT TO TRANSCRIPT OF PROCEEDINGS AND
APPELLATE REVIEW

For several technical reasons, the *Gault* decision did not precisely delineate those rights related to juvenile court reporting procedures:

[13]L. Teitelbaum, "The Use of Social Reports in Juvenile Court Adjudications," *Journal of Family Law,* Vol. 7 (Fall 1967), 430–31.

[14]*In re Gault.*

"It is incumbent upon the Juvenile Court to accompany its waiver order with a statement of the reasons or considerations therefor." As the present case illustrates, the consequences of failure to provide an appeal, to record the proceedings, or to make findings or state the grounds for the juvenile court's conclusion may be to throw a burden upon the machinery for habeas corpus, to saddle the reviewing process with the burden of attempting to reconstruct a record, and to impose upon the juvenile judge the unseemly duty of testifying under cross-examination as to the events that transpired in the hearings before him.[15]

The case cited was *Kent* v. *United States,* one year before Gault. The right to a record is established by implication, but the definition of "record" and how it is obtained is ambiguous. The record is apparently either a juvenile court transcript or a reconstruction of previously unrecorded courtroom events. But, as a practical matter, most jurisdictions require court reporters to record all proceedings in *any* juvenile matter that has even the remotest chance of developing into a question of the child's liberty or physical custody. Also as a practical matter, few if any juvenile court jurisdictions would care to "construct the record" by the alternative procedure.

STANDARDS FOR EVIDENCE

As the juvenile's rights are observed in the jurisdictional phase of a bifurcated court hearing, the process moves toward either *sustaining* or *dismissing* the petition that alleges a minor might have committed an offense. The *Gault* decision, and the later *Winship* decision, excluded virtually all of the "hearsay and opinions" theretofore used in juvenile court proceedings on behalf of the minor. This change from civil court to criminal court standards (from hearsay to "beyond reasonable doubt") means that the decision to sustain or dismiss a juvenile court petition must be based on the same evidence standard as adult criminal court. In effect, then, the testimony of police officers and other witnesses is subject to criminal court standards for evidence.

"In societies that presume the innocence of an accused person until there is *proof* of guilt, the theoretical task of the criminal court is simply to determine the adequacy of evidence—the hard legal issues."[16] Of course, this reduces to the requirement that the juvenile court judge must be as "persuaded of the facts" as an adult court judge or jury. Before a juvenile court petition is found to be true, then, *in contested cases,* the same degree of persuasion is required in the juvenile court as criminal court.

[15] *In re Gault.*

[16] E. Eldefonso, A. Coffey, and J. Sullivan, *Police and Criminal Law* (Pacific Palisades, Calif.: Goodyear Publishing Co., Inc., 1972), p. 135.

NONCONTESTED CASES

Discussion of the minor's rights in juvenile court so far has been from the reference point of a minor (or his parents) who have contested the allegations—who have, in other words, required the police and/or the juvenile probation department to *prove* the allegations of the juvenile court petition.

Confessions and other legally admissible methods of accepting the allegations of the juvenile court petition, of course, eliminate the need for an *adversary* jurisdictional hearing. Nonetheless, as a practical matter, contemporary juvenile courts usually require that even noncontested matters present sufficient evidence to sustain the petition should a confession suddenly be withdrawn. (As I noted in the previous chapter, this becomes a procedural matter for police and probation officers because attorneys frequently either change or join the proceedings after they are underway.)

Needs and the Court Disposition

There are only a few choices for the juvenile court in making a case disposition:

1. Dismiss the case.
2. Declare the minor a ward of the court and return him home on probation.
3. Place him on probation without wardship.
4. Declare him a ward and place him in a foster home, relative's home, or institution.
5. Certain variations of the above, depending on the law of the particular jurisdiction.

Procedurally, once "fact is found," consideration can be given to one or more of these dispositions. It is only *after* a juvenile court petition has been found to be true that the child's needs are considered. "Irrespective of the needs of the child and no matter how glaring these needs may be, before any plan can be implemented, the child must be legally adjudicated delinquent or unruly."[17]

But in terms of disposing of any juvenile case, what are the guidelines? In fact, there are none—only suggested approaches to meeting the child's needs *and* "curing" delinquent behavior. Sadly, none of the panaceas that come in and out of vogue have been of any great assistance to the

[17]W. G. Whitlatch, "Towards an Understanding of the Juvenile Court Process," *Juvenile Justice,* Vol. 23, No. 3 (1972), 3.

juvenile court. What, then, can the juvenile court hope to do in the way
of a disposition that will meet the minor's needs?

The clinical approach of the *parens patriae* juvenile court remains an
influence in the disposition and provides the philosophy, if not the techniques and procedures, for the appropriate disposition. From the frame
of reference of the clinical assessment of causes and remedies, there are
many alternatives, beginning with the behavioral-science-oriented reports and recommendations received by the juvenile court.

Of course, there is a wide variation in terms of who prepares and
submits these reports—juvenile probation officers, psychiatrists, "friends
of the court," social workers, and a host of other sources. But if the
emphasis is on the *value* of the report to juvenile court, it matters little
whether it is submitted by probation officers, private therapists, or social
welfare workers.

> What to do for criminals and delinquents is a perpetual problem, and the
> volume and vigor of opposing views for prevention and treatment indicates
> the absence of reliable knowledge. Several writers have drawn attention to this
> lack of knowledge and have suggested reasons for it, but, with one exception,
> there has been no systematic assessment of specific research studies on the
> effectiveness of various correctional or preventive practices. There have, how-
> ever, been many claims to knowledge or confident policy recommendations in
> both the professional and popular literature. Whatever policies are pursued,
> we would be better off to recognize the extent of our ignorance.[18]

In recognition of the "extent of our ignorance," later chapters will deal
with probation efforts to develop effective alternatives for the juvenile
court disposition. These alternatives emphasize classification and individualized treatment for the juvenile and, in many instances, the family as
well. The goal is even more than the prevention of the recurrence of
delinquency.

> It is fatally easy to treat a delinquent in such a way that the symptom is
> repressed, but the basic urge that caused the anti-social action remains. Smoul-
> dering within, the repressed drive will eventually find an alternative route to
> the surface.
> This alternative route is frequently even more difficult to cure. There is
> little satisfaction in having stopped some criminal behavior with the result that,
> at some later date, the criminal's wife leads a life of hell, or the criminal
> himself, instead of having been sent to prison, is now kept in a mental hospital.

[18]C. H. Logan, "Criminology: Evaluation Research in Crime and Delinquency: A Reap-
praisal," *The Journal of Criminal Law, Criminology and Police Science,* Vol. 63, No. 3
(1972), 378.

The main difference between these two results is that the criminal offends against property and persons, and the lunatic offends against himself. Both kinds of unhappiness are intense. Both kinds of behavior foul the social orbits of those who come in contact with the criminal's misery.[19]

Court disposition geared to the juvenile's needs in this manner goes far beyond the mere processing of delinquency and perhaps approaches the dream of the early *parens patriae* juvenile court. Such an approach opens the door to solutions for *all* of the problems confronting the juvenile court—problems ranging from inadequate resources and staffing to such societal problems as racial difficulties.

While the difficulty of resolving the racial problem is but one of many confronting the juvenile court, it is an example of the value of a dispositional process keyed to the minor's needs. Racial bias is not *usually* a factor in juvenile dispositions. But it does exist. Sensitivity to "our ignorance" and awareness of the goal of matching the juvenile court disposition to the needs of the juvenile, lead to the most effective use of the alternatives available to juvenile court. Presumably, this approach will mitigate the negative effects of a variety of factors which are potentially destructive to the future of the court and the juvenile.

Finally, the two phases of the bifurcated hearing need not be in opposition. The *right* to an adversary hearing, contested at every juncture, in no way reduces the value or lessens the impact of the disposition. Indeed, the juvenile who has violated someone else's rights may be far more receptive to programs that meet his needs if he is convinced that the juvenile court respects the *juvenile's* rights.

Juvenile court is not, and I do not believe it ever was, an experiment. Nor is it unsuccessful, for even those who now shout, as others have shouted over long years for its abolition, only seek to abolish the form. The substance they must retain under some other guise, for it is inherently a part of both nature and law. "As it was in the beginning"—The Code of Hamurabi, or Deuteronomy, if you prefer, "it is now"—the many juvenile codes, for example, the Standard Juvenile Court Act, or the more recent Uniform Juvenile Court Act, "and ever shall be"—either in the courts, or in some administrative agency, say the Youth Service Bureaus.

Let us not deceive ourselves. The problems with which the juvenile courts deal have been with us since man first began to live in organized society, and to promulgate codes of laws. They involve a basic issue, the role of the authority of the state in the life of a child. A few years before the first juvenile court was created, a note in *Lawyers Reports Annotated* says, ". . . but the question

[19]O. L. Shaw, *Youth in Crisis: A Radical Approach to Delinquency* (New York: Hart Publishing Co., Inc., 1966), p. 10.

goes to the very depths of the subject of civil government, and may grow more difficult as the necessity of saving the young from evil lives becomes more pressing or apparent."

No one can dispute that this necessity, forseen 90 years ago, is both pressing and apparent today.[20]

Summary

This chapter presented the juvenile court in transition from the historically derived *parens patriae* approach to an increasing concern with the juvenile's constitutional rights. The *Winship, Kent,* and (especially) *Gault* decisions were discussed as the source of the concern with juvenile rights.

The bifurcated juvenile court hearing was discussed as an approach which separates consideration of factual evidence from consideration of case disposition. Bifurcation was elaborated in terms of adversary jurisdictional hearings, particularly in the case of *contested matters,* as an aspect of juvenile *rights.* The dispositional hearing was presented as an essentially nonadversary phase because of its concern for the juvenile's *needs.*

Ramifications of the *Gault* decision in terms of due process were discussed, as were the ramifications of the 1970 *Winship* decision which clearly established a shift from the civil court "preponderance of evidence" to the beyond-a-reasonable-doubt standard of the criminal court. Also discussed were the juvenile's right to notice, counsel, cross-examination, and protection from self-incrimination. Appellate review with or without a court-recorded transcript was also discussed. Such juvenile court procedures as petition filing were presented as practical applications of some of these rights.

Dispositional considerations were discussed in terms of the alternatives available for delinquents, predelinquents, and waywards. The clinical approach of the *parens patriae* juvenile courts was presented as the basic philosophical context for deciding probation alternatives. The need for dispositions that meet the needs of the minor was stressed.

Questions

1. Explain the transition that the juvenile court is undergoing.
2. Define *bifurcated hearing.*

[20]D. J. Young, "Is the Juvenile Court Successful?", *Federal Probation,* Vol. XXXV, No. 2 (1971), 12.

3. How does the contested case bring about an adversary jurisdictional hearing?

4. Discuss the rights that the *Gault* decision *explicitly* gave juveniles.

5. What right is implied but not explicitly stated in the *Gault* decision?

6. Contrast civil and criminal court standards for evidence.

7. Distinguish between rights and needs in the context of this chapter.

8. Do you think that concern for rights and legality in the first phase of the bifurcated hearing affects concern for needs in the second (dispositional) phase? How?

9. How is the *parens patriae* philosophy expressed today in the dispositional hearing?

10. Bifurcated juvenile court hearings are considered by some to be an experiment. Assuming that this is a valid attitude, explain why you believe the experiment will be dropped *or* accepted as standard procedure.

Annotated References

ARNOLD, W. R., "Race and Ethnicity Relative to Other Factors in Juvenile Court Dispositions," *American Journal of Sociology,* Vol. 77, No. 2 (1971). Raises a great number of questions in the context of this discussion of transition.

CROXTON, T. A., "The Kent Case and Its Consequence," *Journal of Family Law,* Vol. 7, No. 1 (1967).

ELDEFONSO, E., A. COFFEY, and J. SULLIVAN. *Police And Criminal Law.* Pacific Palisades, Calif.: Goodyear Publishing Co., Inc., 1972. Elaboration, in numerous contexts, of due process.

GLEN, J. E., "Bifurcated Hearings in the Juvenile Court," *Crime and Delinquency,* Vol. 16, No. 3 (1970). Well-written exploration of the court distinction between rights and needs.

ROSENHEIM, M. K., *Justice for the Child: The Juvenile Court in Transition.* New York: Free Press, 1962. A good context for considering transition but from the perspective of a decade ago.

YOUNG, D. J., "Is the Juvenile Court Successful?", *Federal Probation,* Vol. XXXV, No. 2 (1971). A realistic, yet encouraging, assessment of contemporary juvenile courts.

9

Detention and Probation

Juvenile detention can occur in two extremely different situations. *Predispositional detention* means that the minor is held in custody until there is a determination of the best alternative course of action. *Dispositional detention,* on the other hand, is the last alternative; that is, the court's ruling is that the juvenile will be detained in either a foster home or some kind of institution. Only the first occasion for detention will be discussed in this chapter.

The National Council on Crime and Delinquency finds few acceptable reasons for predispositional detention.[1] In all cases there must be *specific evidence* that: the minor is "likely to flee" from the jurisdiction; he is likely to commit another offense; or he is in danger of harming himself or others. In the majority of cases, however, it is the police who decide upon initial detention. It should not be surprising, then, that a number of practical considerations influence predispositional detention and that the rationale for detention varies from department to department.

---

[1] *Standards and Guides for the Detention of Children and Youth* (New York: National Council on Crime and Delinquency, 1961).

The small police department, for example, may rarely detain a juvenile simply because it has no facilities for minors. Or, for any department, investigation or interrogation may be more convenient if the juvenile is detained. And there is always the possibility that a juvenile who has not been detained will commit another offense and cause community criticism of the police.

However, the argument against predispositional detention for juveniles is based on the absense of bail: "No bail procedure has been established at the juvenile court level. . . . The reason for this is that a juvenile is not charged with the commission of a crime and therefore is not entitled to . . . bail."[2] An adult can be detained if he is charged with a crime; in most cases he can also be released on bail until the time of his appearance in court. But can someone who has not been charged with a crime (and therefore cannot be released on bail) be detained until the court makes its decision?

> It is estimated that well over 100,000 boys and girls of juvenile court age are held in county jails and police lock ups. . . . Locking children in jails labels them delinquent in advance of a court decision and gives them delinquency status with their peers. It also removes from parent and child responsibility for his behavior in the community pending court disposition. Incarcerating a youngster in jail is not the kind of care, custody, or discipline which a parent ought to have given his child, and which the law says he should have. Even when children are separated from adults in jail, the result is enforced idleness, lack of supervision, physical and sexual aggression, and even teen-age suicides.[3]

But there is a trend toward releasing adults on their own recognizance. That is, an adult who is charged with a crime (unless it is punishable by death) can be released *without* bail unless there is evidence that bail is necessary to insure his subsequent court appearance.

Concern with such inequities between the juvenile and adult justice systems is justified. The philosophy that, whenever possible, the *least restrictive action* should be taken (in regard to juvenile detention, sentencing, and so on) is gaining favor. Least restrictive action emphasizes rehabilitation rather than punishment and, to a great extent, results from Supreme Court concern for juvenile liberty (as reflected in the *Gault* decision). The inequities of juvenile detention are heightened by the fact that, in many cases, juveniles are detained in facilities either designed for adults (and therefore inadequate for juveniles) or below acceptable standards even for the adults for whom they were originally intended.

[2]J. P. Kenny and D. G. Pursuit, *Police Work with Juveniles and the Administration of Juvenile Justice* (Springfield, Ill.: Charles C Thomas, Publisher, 1972), p. 259.

[3]S. Norman, *Proceedings: Juvenile Detention and Community Responsibility*, pamphlet (Austin, Tex.: Texas Women's University, 1968), p. 1.

FACILITIES

The juvenile detention facility is generally known as "juvenile hall" or "the detention home." Detention homes were first created after the passage of the juvenile court law which provided for separate juvenile facilities. At first, these were converted private homes, but the county infirmary, the workhouse, and hospital wings were soon pressed into use as detention facilities. It was in the west, after World War II, that the "juvenile hall," modeled after the large British boarding schools and enclosed within walls, was first constructed.

Neglected and abused children are not sent to juvenile hall, and the *shelter* should not be confused with it. "Shelter is the temporary care of children in physically unrestricted facilities, usually pending return to their own homes or placement for longer term care. . . . Its main use is for dependent and abused children."[4] Delinquents, however, are occasionally detained in a shelter when they are not apt to run away but should not be returned to a poor home situation.

> An initial court-ordered detention in a juvenile hall marks a youth's entry into the correctional system. This appears to be a crucial period in a boy's life. It marks the first time that society judges his behavior to be sufficiently serious and beyond control to require the constraints of an institutional setting; official intervention now takes a rehabilitative rather than merely a socialization function.[5]

It should never be forgotten that this is, indeed, "a crucial period in a boy's life." When he enters a juvenile hall he cannot but be impressed by the fact that adults have decided he must be "locked up." This may be the first time that a child consciously thinks of himself as "bad." Perhaps he is even "dangerous." If his peer group attaches some sort of glamor to these labels, detention serves to increase his status within the peer group. Initial detention, then, may be the occasion for the juvenile to begin thinking of himself as a "criminal." Police and parole officers must always be aware of the effect this conscious or unconscious labeling will have on the individual.

Detention Procedures

After a child has been taken into custody by the police, both police and probation officers become involved in intake procedures (see Chapter 7). The parents are notified by both police and probation officers and the latter discuss with them the alternative courses of action. The juvenile is

[4]*Standards and Guides for the Detention of Children and Youth,* pp. 1–2.
[5]G. G. O'Connar, "The Impact of Initial Detention Upon Male Delinquents," *Social Problems,* Vol. 18, No. 2 (1970), 194.

notified of his rights at the time of his arrest and later by the probation officer. When the probation officer receives a juvenile for detention, he must decide whether to file a petition. At this point, too, the probation officer makes his decision regarding detention. This decision may (in many jurisdictions) be reviewed by the court. Finally, if there is to be a hearing that could result in the juvenile's continued detention, both he and his parents must be notified of the date and possible consequences of the hearing and the nature of the allegations in the petition.

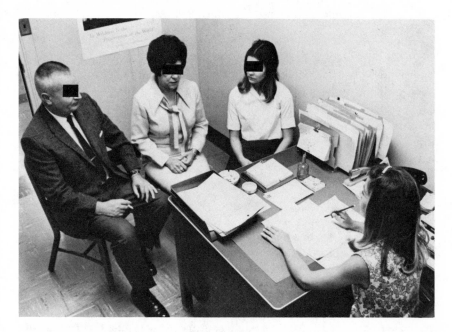

Photo by Charles Tado, County of Santa Clara, California

In other words, police-probation intake procedures must involve both the juvenile and his parents to such a degree that both have a clear idea of the situation. Other procedural matters also occur before disposition of the case, but these will be discussed separately.

Probation

More than fifty years before the creation of juvenile courts, John Augustus, a Boston shoemaker, realized and acted on the need for probation:

> In the month of August, 1841, I was in court one morning, when the door communicating with the lockroom was opened and an officer entered, followed by a ragged and wretched looking man, who took his seat upon the

bench allotted to prisoners. I imagined from the man's appearance, that his offense was that of yielding to his appetite for intoxicating drinks, and in a few minutes I found that my suspicions were correct, for the clerk read the complaint, in which the man was charged with being a common drunkard. The case was clearly made out, but before sentence had been passed, I conversed with him for a few minutes, and found that he was not yet past all hope of reformation. . . . I determined to aid him, I bailed him by permission of the Court. He was ordered to appear for sentence three weeks from that time. He signed the pledge and became a sober man . . . the judge expressed himself much pleased. . . . Instead of the usual penalty . . . he fined him one cent and costs. . . . The man continued industrious and sober . . . saved from a drunkard's grave.[6]

Today, Augustus is known as the Father of Probation, and his efforts on behalf of both adults and juveniles (before there was any judicial separation by age) resulted in the possibility of probation for both. A Chicago law of 1861 authorized the mayor to appoint a commissioner before whom boys between the ages of six and seventeen might appear when charged with petty offenses. Official public control of juvenile probation was established in Massachusetts in 1869. The first juvenile court, as I mentioned previously, was not established until 1899.

> Probation, as it relates to children, may be defined as a system of treatment for the delinquent child, or, in the case of the neglected or destitute child, for delinquent parents, by which the child and parents remain in their ordinary environment and to a great extent at liberty, but, throughout a probation period, subject to the watchful care and personal influence of the agent of the court known as the probation officer.[7]

This description of probation was written in 1918. It is essentially accurate today after more than half a century of social change. But probation has become a concept rather than a procedure for working with juveniles. That is, probation is recognized as a valid alternative to more than detention. One example is unofficial probation: "The primary assumption underlying the use of unofficial probation is that it is at least as effective as formal probation in protecting society from further delinquency. . . . It has been argued that it diverts youngsters from courts, thus avoiding the long-lasting consequences of adjudication such as . . . harm to personal and family reputation and the labeling of children as delin-

[6]J. Augustus, *A Report of the Labors of John Augustus, for the Last Ten Years, in Aid of the Unfortunate* (Boston: Wright and Harty, 1852). Reprinted as *John Augustus: First Probation Officer* (New York: National Probation Association, 1939), pp. 4–5.

[7]C. L. Chute, *Probation in Children's Courts* (Washington, D.C.: U.S. Children's Bureau, 1918), No. 83, p. 7.

quents."[8] While this and other new uses of probation are still relatively untested, some evidence suggests that "informal probation does not result in any greater rate of official delinquency."[9]

Unofficial, or informal, probation may be another effective means of diverting the predelinquent or the beginning delinquent. If so, it will also drastically ease the load of the juvenile court and improve the situation of the adolescent involved with it. The decision to try informal probation obviously must be made with care. But it appears to hold promise as a technique for diversion.

> Probation provides the potential to modify behavior without the attack on dignity that is associated with liberty deprivation. Unlike the prison inmate facing the social reality that his personal behavior forces his removal from the group, the probationer need only focus on modifications required to remain with the group. Sustaining self-respect permits the corrective program to function at the optimum community-adjustment level.[10]

A SEPARATE BRANCH

The organization and administration of probationary procedures are more efficient when separated from court procedures. This does not imply that the two departments should not have an interdependent relationship. But the court and the probation department may, in fact, work at cross purposes. The Constitution guarantees separation of powers within the federal government for good reason. And there are certain similarities between the branches of government and the branches of the judicial system.

The court must make decisions according to the law. Once a juvenile is brought before the court, his alternatives are necessarily limited. One responsibility of the probation department is the recommendation of alternatives to further contact with law enforcement. This does not mean that probation and the court disagree about suitable action or that the juvenile might theoretically be in the center of a tug-of-war between the wishes of the two branches. But the probation department has the power to divert the offender from further judicial contact. This role in itself effectively separates the two departments. It is the difference between roles, not goals, that distinguishes probation and the court.

[8]P. S. Venezia, *Unofficial Probation: An Evaluation of Its Success* (Davis, Calif.: National Council on Crime and Delinquency, 1972), p. 2.

[9]Ibid., p. x.

[10]A. R. Coffey, "Correctional Probation: What Use to Society," *Journal of the California Probation, Parole and Correctional Association,* Vol. 5, No. 1 (1968), 28–30.

Most often, the basic probation law is determined by the state. But each county appoints its own probation staff and administers its own department. Centralized state probation systems, in which one agency administers the system for the whole state, are increasing. There are also attempts to combine state-administered probation and parole agencies, or the probation agency may handle both juvenile and adult probation. But regardless of the approach, county, state, or even municipal probation agencies have a top administrator, generally the chief probation officer.

Most probation officers, as I have stated previously, are not only officers of the court but also peace officers and, in effect, social workers. Their role as peace officers is by no means easy to integrate with the philosophy of least restrictive action. The peace officer's responsibility to protect the community from delinquency may seem at odds with the probation officer's responsibility for finding alternatives to detention. But where strong alternative programs have been developed, it becomes clear that the least restrictive approach does not conflict with the peace officer's responsibility. The police have first-hand evidence that such programs do not encourage delinquency but are an effective force for diversion and control.

The philosophy of least restrictive action does not mean that the police or the community simply turn their backs on the problems of delinquency. It is a philosophy for responsible action founded on the observation that exposure to juvenile court and detention facilities can be "proof" of delinquent identity to many adolescents.

Summary

Predispositional and *dispositional detention* were defined, and acceptable reasons for predispositional detention were outlined. Inconsistencies in juvenile detention standards and inequities between juvenile and adult detention were pointed out. An argument can be made against predispositional juvenile detention on the grounds that there is no bail for juveniles. Such concern for juvenile liberty and emphasis on *least restrictive action* were traced to recent Supreme Court decisions.

After a brief review of detention procedures (described more fully in Chapter 7), the history and conceptual development of probation were traced. Describing philosophical differences between probation and the court, the validity of separating these branches was established.

Finally, the philosophy of least restrictive action was discussed in terms of community protection and police attitudes. It was pointed out that informal probation and similarly "permissive" programs are thoughtful, responsible efforts at rehabilitation which have not proved to be a threat to the public.

Questions

1. Describe the difference between predispositional and dispositional probation.
2. How can the absence of bail contribute to the loss of liberty for juveniles?
3. In your own words, define the least restrictive action philosophy. Outline the case for *or* against this philosophy with respect to juvenile justice.
4. List the acceptable reasons for detaining a juvenile in juvenile hall. If you can think of other valid reasons, list those and explain why you think they should be included.
5. What is the difference between informal and formal probation? Describe the advantages and disadvantages of "deformalizing" judicial procedures.
6. Explain how police and probation officers might work together to rehabilitate juveniles without involving the juvenile court.
7. How might the police and probation officers' responsibilities toward the community conflict with the philosophy of least restrictive action?

Annotated References

COFFEY, A., *Administration of Criminal Justice: A Management Systems Approach.* Englewood Cliffs, N.J.: Prentice-Hall, Inc., 1973. A comprehensive discussion of managerial, fiscal, and administrative benefits in the separation of juvenile probation and juvenile court activities.

COFFEY, A., E. ELDEFONSO, and W. HARTINGER. *Human Relations: Law Enforcement in a Changing Community.* Englewood Cliffs, N.J.: Prentice-Hall, Inc., 1971. A thorough analysis of the rationale for expanding the police and probation role in juvenile justice.

———, *Police-Community Relations.* Englewood Cliffs, N.J.: Prentice-Hall, Inc., 1971. More concise discussion of topic described above.

DRESSLER, D., *Practice and Theory of Probation and Parole.* New York: Columbia University Press, 1959.

ELDEFONSO, E., A. COFFEY, and J. SULLIVAN, *Police and the Criminal Law.* Pacific Palisades, Calif.: Goodyear Publishing Co., Inc., 1972. Exploration of the ramifications of detention, bail, and due process.

O'CONNAR, G. G., "The Impact of Initial Detention Upon Male Delinquents," *Social Problems,* Vol. 18, No. 2 (1970). Good description of the psychological and sociological effects of detention.

112 Detention and Probation

Portune, R., *Changing Adolescent Attitudes Toward Police.* Springfield, Ill.: Charles C Thomas, Publisher, 1971. Discussion of a key area for police-probation collaboration in the utilization of least restrictive action.

Pursuit, D. G., J. D. Gerletti, R. M. Brown, and S. M. Ward, *Police Programs for Preventing Crime Prevention.* Springfield, Ill.: Charles C Thomas, Publisher, 1972. Interesting discussion of a wider community base for police-probation collaboration.

Robinson, S. M., *Juvenile Delinquency: Its Nature and Control.* New York: Holt, Rinehart and Winston, Inc., 1963. Chapters 13–16 describe the development of juvenile probation more extensively than was suitable here.

10

Probation and Treatment

The popular notion of the juvenile probation officer is that he calls at the homes of delinquent children, giving advice to them and their parents and watching out for evidence of repeated offenses. In fact, this stereotyped image is rather accurate, if oversimplified.

Court-ordered probation supervision permits a youth to remain in the community under the supervision and guidance of a probation officer. The juvenile court usually imposes certain conditions on his freedom, however, and arrangements are made for the youth to meet these conditions. The conditions imposed are meant to be constructive, not punitive. They are designed to: prevent repetition of delinquent behavior; prevent long-term involvement in deviant conduct; and assist the youth in achieving his potential as a productive citizen.

Once a juvenile has been placed on probation, the primary responsibility of the probation officer is supervision. Ideally, however, supervision and treatment are combined for an overall program of rehabilitation. Good probation involves much more than just giving the adolescent another chance. The main elements of supervision and treatment are surveillance, casework service, and counseling.

Surveillance has always been and remains an important part of probation. If contact with the youth, his family, his school, and other related individuals is not maintained, the other elements of probation cannot be carried out. If improperly used, surveillance is no more than a veiled threat. Worse, it can duplicate the conditions of delinquency—the "cops-and-robbers" game unwittingly enjoyed by delinquents and criminals alike. Used properly, however, surveillance gives the youth some assurance that society is aware of him and interested in him to the extent that it does not want him to repeat the self-defeating behavior that originally brought him to juvenile court.

Casework service should be provided if necessary during probation supervision. Casework services range from assisting in arrangements for medical or dental care to negotiating summer camping trips, the important consideration always being the stability of the child's environment. The probation officer must first determine the needs and problems of the youth and his family. He then sets up contact between the appropriate community service and the family, doing what he can to assure that the service will be used consistently and effectively.

The *counseling* aspect ties service and surveillance together in applied treatment. The youth and his family may need help in developing "coping skills" and other appropriate behaviors. Help in these areas usually is provided by some kind of specialized treatment.

A Basis for Decision

The key to treatment is the evaluation and diagnosis included in the probation officer's report to the court (see Chapter 7). If it is as accurate and complete as possible, the court has a sound basis for its recommendations. The court decision, backed by its power and authority, has an obvious impact on the juvenile's future. If the power of the court supports a specific treatment program, the possibility for successful probation is greatly enhanced.

Careful investigation and diagnosis include an examination of any influential individuals or subcultures—parents, peers, neighborhood, school, and so on. Some awareness of the youth's value system and perceptions and feelings about his behavior, family, and general situation obviously contributes to both evaluation and diagnosis.

The court order may be thought of as the first step in supervised treatment. Of course, this step is most significant when the judge is able to distinguish individual problems and circumstances, the relative seriousness of the offense, and the alternatives available to different individuals. A classification system which would enable both the court and the probation officer to isolate and identify these factors could facilitate decisions about treatment. While such a system would undoubtedly increase the efficiency and consistency of court decisions, it would also have to take into consideration a number of personality types and their characteristic reactions to and interactions with society.

Which Problem, Which Treatment?

Classification systems often increase the efficiency with which any task can be performed. But efficiency may be accomplished at the risk of something else. If juvenile personality problems are categorized, primary concern, instead of treatment, may be directed toward finding the proper slot for each individual. Once this has been accomplished, there may be a tendency to sit back and let the system take over. The juvenile has been labeled and, from this point, is expected to live up to his label. He runs the risk of being stereotyped, and, likewise, his treatment, progress, and ultimate future will be determined in advance. Care must be exercised to avoid the potential for depersonalization built into any system. The probation officer who relies on classifications for his decisions about treatment programs must remember that a system is a generalization; the individual is specific.

Both the juvenile and adult justice systems are approaching what may be a breakthrough in relating appropriate treatment to the particular problems of specific offenders. While exploration of the wide range of literature on offender classification is not within the scope of this volume, a few excerpts will give some idea of the developments in this area.

> Recent years have brought an increased impetus to thinking about classification systems and typologies of criminals and delinquents. A major force contributing to this development has come from developing research programs. As in other fields, scientific progress in the field of corrections depends on reducing the infinite variety of problems through conceptualizations. In order to attack the problems of the field systematically, research efforts have required some sort of theoretical framework, either focusing on developing an etiology of criminal and delinquent behavior or on charting in an organized fashion the signs, symptoms, or dynamics of patterns covering the universe of offenders.
>
> One of the few agreed-upon facts in the field of corrections is that offenders are not all alike. In spite of this, much of the literature in the field is still written as though offenders *were* all alike. Program prescriptions as well tend to be made in an across-the-board fashion, with increased staff-offender ratios, improved job opportunities, or insight therapy recommended for all. Although some action programs are aimed at specific segments of the heterogeneous

offender population (for example, psychiatric treatment for the emotionally disturbed delinquent), few programs base their goals for intervention and their treatment and management prescriptions on a specified rationale for handling differentially the varieties of offender problems which appear in a correctional setting.

Perhaps a comment should be made with regard to an extreme opposite position taken by some treatment-oriented people who have emphasized the great differences among offenders and have resisted any schematization on the basis of loss of meaningful information about individuals. This position does guard against the mistake of administering the same kind of treatment to any group of offenders, but it does so at the cost of requiring an infinite variety of treatments to fit the uniqueness of each case. This position precludes conceptualizing the complex delinquency problem, developing intervention theories and practices, and instigating research investigation. As such, the position must be rejected.

Theoreticians, practitioners, and researchers increasingly seek some classification system—some meaningful grouping of offenders into categories—which offers (1) a step in the direction of explanatory theory with the resulting aid to prediction which follows from understanding, (2) implications for efficient management and effective treatment decisions, and (3) greater precision for evaluative research.

Those classification approaches having the greatest implications for management practices and treatment strategies were described in some detail, and a cross-classification of these typologies was presented. Six cross-classification bands were identified as running across many of these typological systems. The six bands or offender subtypes were entitled: asocial, conformist, antisocial, manipulator, neurotic, subcultural-identifier, and situational offender. The consistency in the data of several of the typological studies which made the cross-classification possible is an encouraging sign, as are the consistencies in approaches to treatment for the various offender subtypes.

Typologies of offenders represent an important method of integrating the increasing body of knowledge in the field of corrections. Currently, throughout the world there is considerable interest in the possibility of developing, in a systematic way, differential treatment strategies for the various types of offenders.

The treatment-relevant typologies being investigated in the correctional world vary considerably in complexity. One end of the complexity dimension is illustrated by a study conducted by the Corrections Department of the District of Columbia . . . in which the community performance of releases of the Lorton Correctional Complex is being investigated for variations by release type (parolees, "good-time" releases, and expirees). At the mid-range of complexity are groupings of offenders based on etiology or on attitude assessment. The Home Office in England has been attempting to develop a typology based on the nature of the offender's problem. Probation officers identify the client's problems as those of personal inadequacy, psychological disturbance, or social stress. An attempt is then made to show how each type of problem interacts with others, with the treatment given, and with the probability of subsequent reconviction.

The treatment-relevant typology most widely used as a basis for differential programming in community settings is the Interpersonal Maturity Level, or I-level system. This typology, originally developed in the early 1950s in connection with a study of military offenders in the United States, was first reported by Sullivan, Grant (later Warren), and Grant. The original theoretical formulation described a sequence of personality or character integrations in normal childhood development. This classification system focuses upon the ways in which the individual is able to see himself and the world, and the ways he is able to interpret what is happening between himself and others. According to the theory, seven successive stages of interpersonal maturity characterize ego development. They range from the least mature, which resembles the interpersonal reactions of a newborn infant, to an ideal of social maturity which is seldom or never reached. Each of the seven stages, or levels, is defined by a crucial interpersonal problem which must be solved before further progress toward maturity can occur. All persons do not necessarily work their way through each stage, but may become fixed at a particular level. In an adolescent delinquent population, maturity levels range from Maturity Level 2 (or I-level 2) to Maturity Level 5 (I_5). Level 5 is infrequent in the adolescent population but represents a significant proportion of young adult offenders. It should be stressed that interpersonal development is viewed as a continuum. The successive steps, or levels, which are described in the theory are seen as definable points along the continuum.

The conceptualization of the sequence of I-levels represents a general theory of individual development. The *subtypes,* however, have been identified empirically in a delinquent population. Currently this classification system is being used as a basis for differential treatment planning in programs involving juvenile and adult and male and female offenders. Considerable research has been reported on the use of this classification system in differential treatment programs.

Variables, such as intelligence, age, and socioeconomic level predicted interpersonal maturity better for white than for black subjects. These findings would appear to have implications for differential determination of the most successful rehabilitative techniques with white and black offenders.

In summary of the current state of research in the area of classification of offenders, sufficient evidence is available to support the importance of identifying treatment-relevant subgroups in the heterogeneous offender population. Only by some form of grouping is it possible to interpret research findings in treatment studies. Still undetermined, however, is the kind of classification frame of reference most useful in developing differential treatment strategies. Our current state of knowledge with respect to defining the most appropriate treatment strategies for the various subgroupings of offenders is discussed later in this paper.[1]

A comparative table by the same author (pp. 120–21) dramatically illustrates the scope and range of interest in classification. As for I-levels,

[1]M. Q. Warren, *Correctional Treatment in the Community Setting: A Report of Current Research* (Washington, D.C.: National Institute of Mental Health, 1972), (HSM) 72-9129. pp. 1–5.

modifications have already been made in this classification system. For example, it is now believed that delinquency most frequently occurs in children who fall between levels two and four, instead of two and five. Subtypes between the different levels also have been developed.

Some Characteristics of Delinquents at Maturity Levels 2, 3, and 4

Maturity Level 2 (I_2). The individual whose interpersonal understanding and behavior are integrated at this level is primarily involved with demands that the world take care of him. He sees others primarily as "givers" or "withholders" and has no conception of interpersonal refinement beyond this. He has poor capacity to explain, understand, or predict the behavior or reactions of others. He is not interested in things outside himself except as a source of supply. He behaves impulsively, unaware of anything except the grossest effects of his behavior on others.

Subtypes: (1) *Asocial, Aggressive* responds with active demands and open hostility when frustrated. (2) *Asocial, Passive* responds with whining, complaining, and withdrawal when frustrated.

Maturity Level 3 (I_3). The individual who is functioning at this level, although somewhat more differentiated than the I_2, still has social-perceptual deficiencies which lead to an underestimation of the differences among others and between himself and others. More than the I_2, he does understand that his own behavior has something to do with whether or not he gets what he wants. He makes an effort to manipulate his environment to bring about "giving" rather than "denying" response. He does not operate from an internalized value system but rather seeks external structure in terms of rules and formulas for operation. His understanding of formulas is indiscriminate and oversimplified. He perceives the world and his part in it on a power dimension. Although he can learn to play a few stereotyped roles, he cannot understand many of the needs, feelings, and motives of another person who is different from himself. He is unmotivated to achieve in a long-range sense or to plan for the future. Many of these features contribute to his inability to accurately predict the response of others to him.

Subtypes: (3) *Immature Conformist* responds with immediate compliance to whoever seems to have the power at the moment. (4) *Cultural Conformist* responds with conformity to specific reference-group delinquent peers. (5) *Manipulator* operates by attempting to undermine the power of authority figures and/or to usurp the power role for himself.

Maturity Level 4 (I_4). An individual whose understanding and behavior are integrated at this level has internalized a set of standards by which he judges his and others' behavior. He can perceive a level of interpersonal interaction in which individuals have expectations of each other and can influence each other. He shows some ability to understand reasons for behavior, some ability to relate to people emotionally and on a long-term basis. He is concerned about status and respect, and is strongly influenced by people he admires.

Subtypes: (6) *Neurotic, Acting-out* responds to underlying guilt with attempts to "outrun" conscious anxiety and condemnation of self. (7) *Neurotic, Anxious* responds with symptoms of emotional disturbance to conflict produced by feelings in inadequacy and guilt. (8) *Situational Emotional Reaction* responds to immediate family or personal crisis by acting out. (9) *Cultural Identifier* responds to identification with a deviant value system by living out his delinquent beliefs.[2]

There is some doubt as to whether it is safe to assume, on the basis of this classification, that delinquents are necessarily immature. There are too many highly variable factors involved in the decision to place one individual into one category for anyone to be completely certain that the decision is accurate. The variety among correctional systems and their personnel probably means that no system would be adopted by even a majority of probation departments. In any case, the perception and accuracy with which I-Levels and other classifications are used is dependent on individual skills and overall departmental sophistication.[3] Diagnosis without labeling is essential, however, and a uniform method is highly desirable.

Complicating Factors

Unfortunately, because probation personnel are involved with the court and its decisions, the role of the probation officer in treatment may complicate the juvenile's response to treatment.

> Whether probation officer, counselor, or psychotherapist, the mere association with the juvenile court may engender in the delinquent or predelinquent child (and perhaps his parents) a combination of suspicion and fear. The awesome power of the court to divide families cannot be gainsaid.
>
> Authority, then, through its potential to foster suspicion and fear, may also supply a motive or at least a "rationalization" for a child to lie, evade, and *distort.*
>
> The corrective authority vested in the treatment person, or more importantly the client's perception of this authority, distorts the client's response and reactions. This distortion may or may not be consciously contrived. But the greater the authority that is perceived, the greater the probable distortion.
>
> The distortion is actually twofold. First there is the simple modification of response out of deference (or out of defiance) to authority in general that is probably a matter of "differential prestige." As used here, "differential pres-

[2] *The Community Treatment Project After Five Years* (Sacramento, Calif.: California Department of the Youth Authority, 1968), pp. 3–4.
[3] D. C. Gibbons, "Differential Treatment of Delinquents and Interpersonal Maturity Levels Theory: A Critique," *The Social Service Review,* 44, No. 1 (1970), 25.

Table 5
CROSS-CLASSIFICATION OF OFFENDER TYPOLOGIES[a]

Subtypes	Jesness	Hunt	Hurwitz	MacGregor	Makkay	Quay	Reiss	Warren
1. Asocial		Sub I	Type II	Schizophrenic	Antisocial Character Disorder-Primitive Aggressive	Unsocialized-psychopath		I_2
Aggressive	Immature, aggressive							Asocial, aggressive
Passive	Immature, passive				Passive-aggressive			Asocial, passive
2. Conformist		Stage I						I_3
Nondelinquently-oriented	Immature, passive				Antisocial Character Disorder-Organized Passive-aggressive	Inadequate-immature /?Subcultural/	/?Relatively integrated/	Conformist, Immature
Delinquently-oriented	Socialized conformist							Conformist, Cultural
3. Antisocial-manipulator	Manipulator	Stage II	Type III	Autocrat	Antisocial Character Disorder-Organized Aggressive		Defective superego	I_3 Manipulator
4. Neurotic				Intimidated	Neurotic		Relatively weak ego	I_4 Neurotic
Acting-out	Neurotic, acting-out							Neurotic, acting-out
Anxious	Neurotic, anxious Neurotic, depressed							Neurotic, anxious
5. Subcultural-identifier	Cultural delinquent	Stage II	Type I	Rebel	Subcultural	Neurotic-disturbed Subcultural	Relatively integrated	I_4 Cultural identifier
6. Situational		Stage II						I_4 Situational, emotional reaction
Types not cross-classified					Mental Retardate Psychotic			

Subtypes	APA	Argyle	Gibbons	Jenkins and Hewitt	McCord	Reckless	Schrag	Studt
1. Asocial	Passive-aggressive personality	Lack of sympathy					Asocial	Isolate
Aggressive	Aggressive Passive-aggressive		Overly aggressive	Unsocialized aggressive				
Passive								
2. Conformist	Passive-aggressive personality	Inadequate superego			Conformist			Receiver
Nondelinquently-oriented	Passive-dependent		Gang offenders	/?Socialized/			Antisocial	
Delinquently-oriented								
3. Antisocial-manipulator	Antisocial personality	Inadequate superego			Aggressive (psychopathic)	Psychopath	Pseudosocial	Manipulator
4. Neurotic	Sociopathic personality disturbance	Weak ego control			Neurotic-withdrawn	Neurotic Personality	Prosocial	
Acting-out			Joyrider Behavior problems	Overinhibited				Love-seeker
Anxious								
5. Subcultural-identifier	Dyssocial reaction	Deviant identification	Gang offenders	Socialized		Offenders of the moment	Antisocial	Learner
6. Situational	Adjustment reaction of adolescence		Casual delinquent			Eruptive behavior		
Types not cross-classified			Heroin user female delinquent					

[a]Reprinted by special permission of the *Journal of Criminal Law, Criminology and Police Science,* Copyright © 1971 by Northwestern University School of Law, Vol. 62, No. 2.

tige" suggests merely that the feeling and phrasing of answers usually vary with the perceived prestige of the questioner.

The second and more significant aspect of distortion involves the suspicion here of authority confronting . . . a nonvolunteer client often reluctant to concede the desirability of corrective treatment.

It is this very reluctance that in part justifies the position that authoritarian corrective treatment is not only the most appropriate method, it may well be the only means of meeting a delinquent's or a predelinquent's needs.

Psychology and psychiatry have contributed to correctional treatment by noting that once expectancies are developed, there follows a process of selective perception and selective memory in the individual. Of course, this enhances the individual's ability to correlate his expectation with his observations.

Many, if indeed not most delinquents and predelinquents bring to correctional treatment the expectation that authority will be threatening. Authority used in an arbitrary manner . . . may reinforce such expectation of threat. Avoiding authority through embarrassment with its potential at best fails to motivate the client towards concern for the consequences of his behavior and at worst fosters contempt for societal regulation of behavior. No authority at all makes correctional treatment virtually impossible or at most optional . . . to clients often reluctant to acknowledge any responsibility for the problem confronting the court.[4]

Determining the nature of treatment is in itself difficult. Even the sophisticated classification system cannot always take into account the subtle variations in the individual juvenile's needs. "It often requires the most careful clinical judgment to know when a particular disturbance in an adolescent's life situation can be approached directly and when handling of it must be deferred until certain crucial changes have been brought about in his characteristic mode of operation."[5]

Furthermore, there are numerous treatment methods, and combinations of methods, from which to choose. Although most methods frequently are believed to work equally well over a broad population, many individuals, in fact, respond more readily to one method (or one type of method) than others. Matching individuals and methods adds to the complexity of treatment planning. Furthermore, there is even more variability in the application of one method by different probation officers than there is in the number of methods. This variability in application relates to skills, caseload sizes, and similar pragmatic considerations.

[4]A. R. Coffey, "The Use of Authority with Delinquents and Predelinquents," Staff Development Division, Santa Clara County Juvenile Probation Dept., Training Bulletin No. 23, pp. 4–6.

[5]H. B. Peck and V. Bellsmith, *Treatment of the Delinquent Adolescent* (New York: Family Service Associations of America, 1954), p. 27.

Descriptions of several treatment methods and a general idea of the kinds of problems dealt with are given in Chapter 2. Although treatment concepts will not be discussed in the following chapter on correctional institutions, there is at least as great a need for treatment within the institution as there is in probation supervision.

Summary

Whereas the previous chapter described probation in its relation to predispositional detention, the focus in this chapter was the relationship between probation and treatment. The importance of providing the court —whose order may be viewed as the initial step in treatment—with sufficient information for a constructive recommendation was pointed out.

Pertinent to court orders is the need for a system of classifying offenders and simplifying the means of providing treatment appropriate to the individual. The advantages and possible disadvantages of classification systems were described, and the interpersonal maturity (I-level) system was reviewed as an example of classification.

The probation officer's authoritarian image was mentioned as a complicating factor in treatment. That is, the response of the juvenile and his family to an authority figure may influence their response to treatment. Nevertheless, the chapter ended by emphasizing the importance of treatment during not only probation but institutional detention and parole.

Questions

1. Describe the probation officer's supervisory duties during probation.
2. Explain how surveillance might be perceived positively and negatively by the juvenile offender.
3. How can a classification system simplify one responsibility of the juvenile court? Explain how you think the juvenile offender can benefit from a classification system.
4. Refer to the description of I-levels. Can you describe yourself and/or any friends or relatives in terms of I-level? If so, does the I-level completely describe the individual or individuals you have in mind? If not, can this inadequacy be explained by the fact that they are not juvenile delinquents? Whether or not you find the description complete, outline your thoughts on classification systems and labeling.
5. Describe your reactions to advice from authority figures (parents, teachers, and so on) and friends (of whatever age). What are the implications of your reactions for the relationship between the parole officer and the juvenile offender?

Annotated References

The following references provide a variety of views on classification systems in general or descriptions of specific systems. See references at the end of Chapter 2 for readings on treatment methods.

BUTLER, E. W., and S. N. ADAMS, "Typologies of Delinquent Girls: Some Alternative Approaches," *Social Forces,* 44 (1966), 401–7.

CALIFORNIA YOUTH AUTHORITY, *The Community Treatment Project After Five Years.* Sacramento, Calif., 1968.

————, *The Status of Current Research in the California Youth Authority.* Sacramento, Calif., 1968.

FERDINAND, T. N., *Delinquent Behavior.* Englewood Cliffs, N.J.: Prentice-Hall, Inc., 1970.

————, "Problems of Causal Analysis in Criminology: A Case Illustration," *Journal of Research in Crime and Delinquency,* 3 (1966), 301–8.

————, *Typologies of Delinquency.* New York: Random House, Inc., 1966.

GIBBONS, D. C., "Differential Treatment of a Delinquent and Interpersonal Maturity Level Theory: A Critique," *The Social Service Review,* Vol. 44, No. 1 (1970).

GOUGH, H., "Theory and Measurement of Socialization," *Journal of Consulting Psychology,* 24 (1960), 23–30.

HARTJEN, C. A., and D. C. GIBBONS, "An Empirical Investigation on a Criminal Typology," *Sociology and Social Research,* 54 (1966), 56–62.

JESNESS, C., "Typology and Treatment," *California Youth Authority Quarterly,* 19 (1966), 17–29.

JOHNS, D. A., J. K. TURNER, and J. W. PEARSON, *Community Treatment Project, An Evaluation of Community Treatment for Delinquents: Seventh Progress Report, Part I, The Sacramento-Stockton and the San Francisco Experiments.* Sacramento, Calif.: Dept. of the Youth Authority, 1968.

LERMAN, P., "Evaluative Studies of Institutions for Delinquents: Implications for Research and Social Policy," *Social Work,* 13 (1968), 55–64.

PRESIDENT'S COMMISSION ON LAW ENFORCEMENT AND ADMINISTRATION OF JUSTICE, *Task Force Report: Corrections.* Washington, D.C.: U.S. Gov't. Printing Office, 1967.

SULLIVAN, C., M. Q. GRANT, and J. D. GRANT, "The Development of Interpersonal Maturity: Applications to Delinquency," *Psychiatry,* 20 (1957), 373–85.

UNITED STATES DEPARTMENT OF HEALTH, EDUCATION AND WELFARE, *Typological Approaches and Delinquency Control: A Status Report.* Washington, D.C., 1967.

WARREN, M. Q., "Classification of Offenders as an Aid to Efficient Management and Effective Treatment," *Journal of Criminal Law, Criminology and Police Science,* Vol. 62, No. 2 (1971).

11

Correctional Institutions
and Parole

Perhaps the most significant factor in any contemporary account of the juvenile correctional institution is its changing population. The lower national birth-rate, lower voting age, and the greater number of juveniles who, for a variety of reasons, are diverted from detention obviously contributed to the decreased correctional institution population. But increased alternatives to detention mean that only those for whom no other alternative can be found are now sent to institutions.

More meaningful than the smaller number of juveniles in these facilities, then, is the increasing tendency to severe behavior problems among those now committed. It is a victory for juvenile justice as a whole, of course, that fewer and fewer children need be detained in institutions. But, for the institution itself, the concentration of severely disturbed youth presents a significant problem. Parole, which is a condition of institutional detainment, obviously is affected by the problems and goals of the correctional facility and will be discussed here in that context.

Nationwide, there are about 50,000 juvenile delinquents in publicly-financed correctional institutions at any given time.[1] This is about 195 out of every 100,000 children between the ages of ten and seventeen.

---

[1] Children's Bureau Statistical Service, *Statistics on Public Institutions for Delinquent Children* (Washington, D.C., 1969), No. 94.

Regionally, however, this ratio varies:[2]

Table 6

Pacific	341 per 100,000
Mountain	205 per 100,000
West Southern Central	192 per 100,000
West Northern Central	183 per 100,000
East Northern Central	166 per 100,000
East Southern Central	188 per 100,000
South Atlantic	238 per 100,000
Middle Atlantic	121 per 100,000
New England	160 per 100,000

The financial cost of operating these correctional institutions also varies regionally:[3]

Table 7

	Per $10,000 Income	Expense per Juvenile
Pacific	$5.51	$4,476
Mountain	4.02	3,607
West North Central	2.55	2,595
West South Central	2.54	2,045
East North Central	2.44	3,669
East South Central	2.43	1,929
South Atlantic	4.41	2,682
Middle Atlantic	2.05	4,824
New England	2.87	4,111

These cost variations can be attributed to such factors as salary scales and the quality and number of correctional services provided. On the average, there are about 2.2 juveniles for every full-time institutional employee.

Minors committed to publicly-operated correctional institutions stay for an average of 8.7 months, which breaks down as follows:[4]

Table 8

City and county juvenile institutions	10.1 mos. avg.
State operated correctional institutions	9.3 mos. avg.
Forestry camps	6.9 mos. avg.
Reception/diagnostic centers	2.5 mos. avg.

In addition to publicly funded and operated institutions, there are many private institutions in which about 7,000 minors are living at any

[2]L. T. Jackson and D. Ligons, *Statistics on Public Institutions for Delinquent Children* (Washington, D.C.: Children's Bureau Statistical Service, 1968), No. 80, p. 4.

[3]Ibid., p. 6.

[4]Ibid., p. 5.

given time.[5] Some believe that this figure is inaccurate since it does not reflect the number of juveniles who have been placed in military academies and similar private institutions as the result of unofficial agreements between parents and judges or probation officers. Most correctional institutions, unlike the juvenile hall, which is ordinarily a holding facility, are geared to "long-term" detention. But, as Table 8 indicates, long-term juvenile detention is usually less than a year. The different correctional institutions discussed in this chapter vary from the large state training school to the foster home and, for the most part, are distinguished here by the kind of treatment they offer, their size, and the problems they can best remedy.

Before proceeding, and to avoid confusion, I would like to make a distinction between correctional institutions and reception and diagnostic centers. Many states operate institutions geared to *assessing* the nature of delinquent behavior problems. Diagnostic centers delineate subsequent treatment programs, but few of them offer treatment and, therefore, are not included in the following discussion.

The Training School

The first training school (or reform school) was probably the Lyman School for Boys, which was opened in 1846 in Massachusetts. The New York Agricultural and Industrial School was established in 1849 and the Maine Boys Training Center in 1853. Today, there is at least one training facility in each state and most are administered by the state government.

The training school, where the child is retrained in custody and various programs of psychotherapy, education, and vocational training are presented to him, would appear to be the institution where the causalities of juvenile delinquency can be scientifically probed and the solutions offered by society's professionally qualified specialists in various fields of the behavioral sciences. . . . [But] training schools provide services that rank among the most difficult to administer and evaluate in the entire field of child welfare: they deal with successive waves of delinquent children, whose stay is often a term of a few months, and they operate with budgetary and staff limitations along with overcrowded and all too often plant facilities too obsolescent to incorporate enlightened programming. . . . Experts have recommended that 150 inmates is a desirable maximum for any institution of delinquents and no more than thirty in cottages. More than one-third of the training schools have been designed to house above two hundred residents and most training schools exceed their quota by sometimes housing twice their allowable maximum.[6]

[5]U.S. Dept. of Commerce, *Statistical Abstract of the United States* (Washington, D.C., 1970).

[6]C. M. Unkovic and W. J. Ducsay, "Objectives of Training Schools for Delinquents," *Federal Probation,* Vol. 33, No. 1 (1969), 49.

Such conditions undoubtedly influence the successes of these institutions. Of those juveniles who finish their detention period in a typical public training school, 25 to 50 percent return for other offenses. If the role of the training school is to "correct" and "rehabilitate," this percentage of returnees indicates how poorly these goals are being met.

Reprinted by permission from *Impact,* Vol. 1, No. 2 (1973).

"The judge said I was neglected. What did you do to be sent here?"

The general failure of the training school is almost universally admitted. It would seem, then, that resistance to change would be low and that there would be considerable motivation to try new programs. But the very factors that plague the present training school system (inadequate facilities, low salaries, staff shortages, and bureaucratic rigidity) also affect the number and scope of possible changes. Innovative programs can be funded and instituted, but the changes they are hoped to effect can be little more than superficial if basic conditions are unsatisfactory.

In Massachusetts, in fact, training schools were discontinued, and those delinquents are now referred to smaller treatment centers in the nearby community.

> The change from institutional to community care for youth . . . came about because this State, although well intentioned, was failing to effectively rehabilitate the juveniles adjudged legally delinquent. . . . Recidivism studies . . . revealed more than a 70 percent return rate of reform school graduates. . . . Institutions failed for reasons inherent in their aims and operation. Their primary role was custodial. . . . The expenditure of energy to keep the children confined, orderly, and obedient left practically no time for the requisite amount of individual attention and ensured that the children's problems would not be resolved. This built-in futility engendered frustration in staff and bitterness in the youth, and created new problems. This "treatment" became for many children the first step in criminal careers.[7]

The sweeping changes that were recommended were not accomplished without difficulty. Administrative and policy modifications were resisted; the "old guard" disagreed with the attitudes of newer and often younger staff. But the state, on its part, resisted the temptation to hope that, with time, change would evolve on its own, that attitudes and policies would become more enlightened, and that communities would voluntarily organize their own treatment centers. The large institutions were shut down. Regional programs were forced to expand; new residential and nonresidential facilities were created. Today, each regional office must identify, develop, and support the necessary services for its own youth.

Resistance to change is difficult to pinpoint. Few people will admit that they like an existing situation when it is being criticized. But the resistance is there—in the defense of one procedure, perhaps, or the argument that something else is to blame and should be changed. Subtle resistance is difficult to overcome. Perhaps many states, already recognizing the expense and inefficiency of outmoded institutions, must follow the example of Massachusetts and force the creation of small, community-run treatment centers as a means of insuring the rehabilitation of delinquents.

[7]Y. Bakal, "The Massachusetts Experience," *Delinquency Prevention Reporter,* April 1973, 1–3.

Camps and Ranches

Ranches and forestry camps may be run by the county or the state. Their programs, size, and so on vary, but their common purpose, unlike the training school, "is to maintain the delinquent child as a part of the community during his treatment process. Contacts with home and family are encouraged, and other normal community interests are sustained. The court is able to review the rehabilitation program it has ordered. Probation officers can counsel with the child and his family before, during, and after his stay."[8]

Training and counseling programs at the camp or ranch work together to modify attitudes and behavior and strengthen the child's self-control. Both elements of treatment are crucial. The training program may be successful in teaching the juvenile constructive behavior patterns, but it alone cannot insure that, once returned to the community, he will have the confidence and control to retain these behaviors. During the counseling process, he may reach some understanding of the value in following camp and, eventually, other rules.

The camp or ranch, like any facility, is more suited to some juveniles than others. Severely disturbed youths, for example, probably will not profit from such an environment because they will lack the required, although minimal, self-control. These facilities, however, can be tailored to the needs of more than one segment of the delinquent population. The severely disturbed juvenile, too, should be given opportunities to test himself. Even a diagnosis which seems to limit institutional and personal goals is not an excuse to say "no" to opportunities for growth.

Halfway Houses and Day Care

Halfway houses are more common to adult than juvenile corrections. But certainly the halfway house can be a suitable alternative to the larger institution or even probation for many delinquents. The Denver juvenile court has developed two such houses which are typical of the few so far in existence. One is for boys, the other for girls. The age range is from twelve to fourteen-and-one-half years. Fifteen children initially were placed in each six-month program, but this is now believed to be too many. The Denver program offers education, counseling, and group interaction (for children *and* their parents).

Halfway houses, of course, need a responsible and responsive staff. Furthermore, the juveniles who are referred to such programs must be capable of enough self-control and responsibility to respect the relative

[8]V. Roley, *Planning Local Rehabilitation Programs for Juvenile Offenders* (Sacramento, Calif.: California Youth Authority, 1965), pp. 5–7.

freedom of the halfway house. Such considerations may explain some of the reluctance toward establishing more of these facilities for children. Adult halfway houses, too, are an intermediary step between the serving of a sentence and the regular parole period. Because juveniles are ordinarily paroled to their parents' care, the halfway house may seem an unnecessary and wasteful operation. But juvenile halfway houses need not duplicate those for adult criminals. They can be used instead of more restrictive detention, for example, for children whose home situation needs improvement before they can be put on probation.

The day-care facility is a similar alternative. There are many juveniles who, for a variety of reasons, will not do well on probation but do not need institutional commitment. Day care offers them a kind of intensive probation, because they must report daily for an educational treatment program.

Day care and halfway houses, then, provide further alternatives to the training school. Such facilities, which offer intensive treatment but are limited to a few children, will become more common as communities assume more responsibility for all their residents—not only delinquents but the retarded, mentally ill, and other "problems" who have been sent miles from home and family to large and, too often, inadequate institutions.

Foster Homes

Most juvenile courts have direct access to foster homes in which dependent children can be placed if they are likely to receive continued neglect or abuse in their own home. Unfortunately, the need for good foster homes has almost always exceeded the supply. This is even more frequently the case as more delinquent children are referred to foster homes. Even in jurisdictions which offer adequate compensation, it is difficult to find couples who are willing and able to cope with delinquent wards of the court.

Nevertheless, when qualified foster parents can be found, the care, control, and guidance they can provide, usually missing in the original home, often insure successful rehabilitation. In these cases, the probation officer and foster parents often form what amounts to a treatment team until the juvenile can be returned to his own home. In this context, the foster home is certainly correctional—if not institutional—and in many cases provides perhaps the best elements of any treatment program— close personal attention, understanding, and sympathetic firmness about the necessity of following "family" rules.

Private institutions, referred to earlier in the chapter, usually adopt the same team approach as the foster parent with the probation officer. The object, again, is to encourage personal and family growth.

The Goal of Treatment

While much is said about the complexity of treating the problems of any juvenile and the fallacy in assuming that there is a simple remedy, simplistic approaches are all too common. Change is always difficult, even when there is a desire for it. And with the child it is even more difficult, for he has much less control over his environment than the adult. Dramatic external change can sometimes bring about at least some degree of internal change. An adult may get a divorce, change jobs, move to another city—start over. Children often are not provided with such opportunities. And yet, the probation officer, social worker, or psychologist cannot hope to change the child *and* his family *and* his peers *and* his neighborhood. He must somehow help the child cope with what is almost always a difficult situation in which the child is, in effect, the only variable.

When a child is detained in a correctional institution, he must be given opportunities to try out alternative behaviors. Surrounded by staff who have no *real* expectation of change and therefore provide no opportunities for it, the delinquent knows that the only expectation he can fill is his own delinquency. Few people will immediately conform to new expectations, but everyone needs to see that different choices *can* obtain different results.

The delinquent in a correctional institution must: understand what behavior is expected of him and of others in that situation; understand the consequences of both violating and accepting these expectations; understand what he loses and what he gains in either case; perceive a real difference in the two alternatives; understand his role in the consequences; and understand that, ultimately, no one controls his role but himself. Treatment means correction only if it goes beyond diagnosis and theoretical remedies to active, consistent, open-minded programs to awaken and encourage individual responsibility.

Parole

Parole, like most other aspects of the juvenile justice system, is not governed by a set of nation-wide standards. Parole supervision may be handled by any one of several agencies: the training school; the juvenile court; a state agency; a public or private casework agency; the adult parole authority; the judge; or volunteer organizations. The release of a youth from a correctional institution and his adjustment should be gradual. One weak part in the rehabilitation process is the supervision of paroled youth. Few parole staffs are large enough or well enough trained to handle postinstitutional training problems.

Reprinted by permission from *Impact,* Vol. 1, No. 2 (1973).

Stigma Cum Laude

Nevertheless, like probation supervision, parole supervision attempts to combine supervision and treatment as a means of returning the offender to his family and community. Unlike the juvenile on probation, however, the delinquent who is released on parole from an institution has a delinquent identity. Whether this identity is perceived as a status symbol or a stigma, it poses the greatest challenge to treatment and rehabilitation. The delinquent, usually isolated from outside influences for several months, emerges from the institution with a label and a sense of alienation. Both of these may be a source of pride to him, but nevertheless they are a significant barrier to his rehabilitation and reintegration with the community.

This difference between the juvenile on probation and the paroled delinquent means that treatment orientation must also differ. Otherwise, however, treatment methods are very similar, and the two programs can and often do share the same staff. (Chapter 2 offers a review of many of the treatment methods used by probation and parole programs.)

THE PAROLE BOARD

The parole board determines whether the offender can be released on parole and, frequently, if parole is to be revoked. "For juvenile offenders, the law permits the utmost flexibility. Discharge [release from parole supervision] may come soon after release or it may not be granted until majority [adult status] has been attained."[9]

Because parole programming formally begins with the parole board, it is significant that this body, too, is undergoing change. As institutional treatment, parole board review, and parole treatment coordinate their concerns for and work with the delinquent, the chances for successful "prerelease" programs improve. Prerelease recommendations may vary from parole to the home, to a halfway house or similar agency, to transfer to another state. (The last alternative, arranged by *interstate compact,* allows the paroled delinquent to be released under the supervision of a parole officer in another state and transferred to a foster home or relative's home in that state.)

The parole board's initial decision and recommendation are based, at least partially, on the delinquent's behavior and progress within the institution. The degree of communication between the individual delinquent, the institutional staff, and the parole board is obviously important. Ideally, of course, the overall institutional program is geared to prerelease. Family and community problems should be anticipated and worked on during the delinquent's detention, and by the time he is considered for parole, the board should have a fairly accurate basis for deciding the terms of his parole.

RELATED RESPONSIBILITIES

The responsibilities of the training school and parole officer are tremendous:

> Our goal is to take every girl, no matter how antagonistic she may be, and within six to eight months rehabilitate her so that, with the guidance of a parole officer, she will be able to stay out of further serious trouble in the community. Naturally, we do not succeed with everyone. . . . Since the total program for all girls includes both custody and parole, the return of a girl to the institution is not necessarily an indictment of our efforts. . . . As often as possible the parole officer is given definite recommendations for the best way to handle the girl. . . . It is important that I do not give the impression that the school does the whole job. A dedicated parole officer is necessary to continue guiding the girl toward a successful life in the community.[10]

[9]D. Dressler, *Practice and Theory of Probation and Parole* (New York: Columbia University Press, 1959), pp. 67–68.

[10]W. Glasser, *Reality Therapy: A New Approach to Psychiatry* (New York: Harper & Row, Publishers, 1965), p. 68.

This is a description of a training school for girls with a return rate of about 20 percent, relatively low when compared with the national average (25 to 50 percent). Even the best institutions, however, can accomplish only a limited amount in six to eight months. And who shares the parole officer's responsibility "for guiding the delinquent toward a successful life in the community"?

"Scattered here and there across the country are impressive new school programs designed to help children in trouble."[11] The irony implicit in this evaluation would be recognized by the many parole officers across the country who have found their efforts to return a juvenile to school emphatically rejected by school officials. Most parole officers strongly believe that an effective educational program enhances the delinquent's chances for success during parole.

But the fear that paroled delinquents mean only trouble to students and staff alike prevents many school officials from organizing educational programs for the delinquent's benefit or even allowing him to pursue the regular course of study. Perhaps toleration for and concern with the parolee will increase as school personnel become aware of the extent of some forms of delinquency (for example, drug abuse) in the schools.

The ideal, of course, is education without further reinforcement of the delinquent identity—without segregated "delinquent schools." Successful reentry and readjustment to the community certainly requires a level of education not usually achieved at the time most delinquents are confined to an institution. But, until community enlightenment is advanced, specialized educational programs of some sort must be included in parole treatment.

Parole, as rehabilitative "after-care," is in every sense society's last chance to prevent many delinquents from becoming the adult criminals whose careers are an unbelievable expense in terms of money, lives, suffering, property loss, and general fearfulness. Unfortunately, however, parole is the weakest link in the juvenile justice system. It cannot continue to provide, as it does in many cases, the delinquent's means of access to a career as an adult criminal.

Prevention, diversion, and probation programs channel many juveniles away from such a career. Certainly these programs should not be deemphasized in the process of improving the parole system. As a branch of corrections, parole might profit by adopting the following outlook:

Two general movements can be observed in current correctional treatment research. Both of these call for increasing differentiation of the "who" and the "what" of correctional programs. The "who" question involves a greater

[11]H. James, *Children in Trouble* (Boston: Christian Science Publishing Society, 1969), p. 81.

concern with the characteristics of the offender which brought him into a correctional system, as well as the relationship between those characteristics and what will be required to get him out of the correctional system permanently.[12]

Summary

Significant to a discussion of corrections and parole is the decreasing population of the institution and the concentration of juveniles with severe behavior problems in this population. Types of correctional facilities were reviewed and described, and the problems involved in treating the institutionalized juvenile were brought out.

Parole from the institution was described as society's chance for successful rehabilitation but the weakest link in juvenile justice. Differences between parole and probation treatment were described as minimal, the chief variable being the orientation of the former to the "confirmed" delinquent. Generally, discussion of parole emphasized the need for cooperation and communication between institutional treatment staff, parole board, parole officer, and influential community services (for example, the school) in order to insure the delinquent's successful reentry into nondelinquent society.

Questions

1. Compare and relate: juvenile hall; probation; training school; and parole.
2. Describe the type of correctional facility which you think affords the best chance for juvenile rehabilitation. Explain your choice.
3. Explain the difficulties involved in treating the juvenile while he is institutionalized in the training school. List any ideas you have for minimizing or eliminating these difficulties.
4. How large or small a role do you think the community should take in the rehabilitation of delinquents? Explain, including what rehabilitation means to you.

Annotated References

ALLEN, T. E., "An Innovation in Treatment at a Youth Institution," *Federal Probation*, Vol. 33, No. 1 (1969). Exploration of the program latitude in training schools.

CARY, L., *Work Camps for Young Offenders*. Syracuse, N.Y.: Syracuse University Press, Youth Development Center, 1960.

[12]M. Q. Warren, *Correctional Treatment in Community Settings* (Washington, D.C.: National Institute of Mental Health, 1972), Publication No. (HSM) 72–9129, p. 51.

ELIAS, A., "Innovations in Correctional Programs for Juvenile Delinquents," *Federal Probation,* Vol. 33, No. 4 (1968). Provides good understanding of the impact of both training school and probation treatment upon juveniles.

HARTINGER, W., E. ELDEFONSO, and A. COFFEY, *Corrections: A Part of Criminal Justice.* Pacific Palisades, Calif.: Goodyear Publishing Co., Inc., 1973. Comprehensive treatment of the entire correctional process.

JACKSON, L. T., and D. C. LIGONS, *Statistics on Public Institutions for Delinquent Children.* Washington, D.C.: Children's Bureau, Social and Rehabilitation Service, 1967. Excellent statistical background for this chapter. See also: *Statistical Abstract of the United States,* Washington, D.C.: U.S. Dept. of Commerce.

UNKOVIC, C. M., and W. J. DUCSAY, "Objectives of Training Schools for Delinquent," *Federal Probation,* Vol. 33, No. 1 (1969). An exceptionally clear delineation of training school objectives.

12

The Future
of Juvenile Court

The future of juvenile court holds as many uncertainties as probabilities—but predictions are a singularly risky business. This chapter, nevertheless, will explore and assess some of the probabilities, beginning with the numbers of children who may be involved.

As mentioned in the previous chapter, the birth rate in America is declining and currently at an all-time low.[1] This does not necessarily mean that fewer juveniles will be involved with juvenile court. Indeed, it is conceivable that the numbers coming before the juvenile court could increase if, for example, delinquency prevention and diversion were to fail and if larger percentages of youth become involved in delinquency.

But the lowered voting age is another factor. The Congressional decision to reduce the voting age to eighteen for national elections was followed by a similar reduction in voting age in many states. In effect,

[1]U.S. Census Bureau revision of a projected population (by the year 2000) of 330 million downward to 280 million, based on a special 1972 update of 1970 census statistics.

then, there are more adults and fewer juveniles, and juvenile court jurisdiction has been sharply reduced.

This decline affords a context for several other probabilities that will
be explored in this chapter.

Before exploring the context of "more service through fewer referrals," however, brief consideration should be addressed to the idea that
there should be *no* future for juvenile court: "In fact, not only is truancy,
running away and incorrigibility none of the court's business, it may be
that in the future nothing a child does (under a certain age) is the business
of the court. Other answers will be found and other services provided,
thereby permitting the courts to do what they are supposed to do,
namely, protecting adults from killing each other."[2]

Fewer Referrals: More Service

Assuming that juvenile courts *will* deal with fewer children in the
future, what will this mean to the juvenile justice system? Considering
only the question of juvenile court service, there are at least two alternatives: reduce staffing and services in direct proportion to the decline in
referrals, or increase the services in direct proportion to the reduction in
referrals. The staffing and services referred to are primarily those of
probation, which has been presented as a function apart from the juvenile
court. But the two subsystems interact so closely that change in one
affects the other.

A convincing argument could be made for reducing court resources in
proportion to the volume of referrals *if* the juvenile court were able to
demonstrate any overwhelming success at this ratio. Pursuing this alternative, of course, would perpetuate the court's regrettably insufficient
impact upon juvenile delinquency. If this failure is acknowledged, the
only acceptable alternative is an increase in services as referrals decrease.
This does not mean, however, that there is necessarily a need for more
of the *same* services. It *does* mean increasing application of "new ideas,
new answers, and adjustment to changing social problems."[3]

Increasing service means taking into account many long-standing and
serious problems: "A juvenile may get nothing more than a mattress on
the floor of an antiquated, overcrowded detention facility, and in some
juvenile institutions there are indignities, solitary confinement, physical
punishment, and intentional degradations."[4]

[2]"Juvenile Court Overreach," *Impact,* Vol. 1, No. 2 (1973), 2.
[3]O. W. Ketcham, "The Juvenile Court for 1975," *Social Service Review,* Vol. XL, No.
3 (1966), p. 288.
[4]Ibid.

This, then, is one aspect of the court's future—fewer youths but increasingly effective services. "The juvenile court has always had its critics, but not until recent years have its theoretically benevolent purposes come under sustained attack. Recent decisions of the Supreme Court have questioned whether the court treats children humanely enough to justify its immunity from the safeguards of criminal law."[5]

Supreme Court Influence

One of the great virtues of our Constitutional system is that it is not static; it has dynamic powers of adjustment, recovery, and self-correction. When the legislators fail to respond to pressing problems, those problems often are pressed on the courts. And judges must fashion remedies if the law so provides. One of the beneficial results of some of the controversial decisions of the last 15 years, laying aside debate over whether the Constitution supports them, is that they focused attention on the need for action by local governments and police. The police, short on money and trained leadership, turned to Congress and we now have the Law Enforcement Assistance Administration providing money and training to improve police practices. With that kind of support and the guidance of experts in various fields, there has been a marked improvement in police operations.[6]

These comments afford some philosophical insight into at least part of the rationale for such decisions as *Kent, Gault,* and *Winship.* And in terms of the future of juvenile court the opening statement is particularly significant.

Change relates not only to social factors but to the Constitutional system itself, and the Supreme Court may prove to be more than "not static"—a systematically significant force whenever "the legislators fail to respond to pressing problems."[7]

Future juvenile courts almost certainly will retain at least as much sensitivity to the Supreme Court's Constitutional interpretations as they have since the *Gault* decision. Even when the legislators respond to pressing problems, "there is the . . . risk that public interest, now at a peak, will again falter unless intelligent efforts to achieve minimum standards of juvenile justice are quickly initiated."[8]   The Supreme Court,

---

[5]R. M. Mennel, "Origins of the Juvenile Court: Changing Perspectives on the Legal Rights of Juvenile Delinquents," *Crime and Delinquency,* Vol. 18, No. 1 (1972), 69, citing Mr. Justice Fortas, *Kent* v. *U.S.,* 383 U.S. 541, 545 (1966).

[6]W. E. Burger, "The Chief Justice Talks About the Court," *Readers' Digest* (Feb. 1973), 99.

[7]Ibid., p. 99.

[8]J. F. X. Irving, "Juvenile Justice—One Year Later," *Journal of Family Law,* Vol. 8, No. 1 (1968), 1.

therefore, has the ultimate responsibility for dealing with pressing problems, and when legislators reflect peaking and faltering public interest, it is the Supreme Court which will intervene in the interest of juvenile justice. While it is difficult to forecast the precise form that such intervention may take, the current trend toward adversary hearings seems a probable format.

Bifurcated Hearings

Although we have discussed bifurcated hearings in their present context of contested petitions, it is likely that future juvenile courts will be required to bifurcate all hearings. The current focus upon the possible loss of liberty in unbifurcated hearings will probably intensify to the point that the change is made. This is not to suggest that there will be an accompanying reduction of emphasis on needs during the dispositional phase. To the contrary, as you have read, probation services are likely to expand dramatically in the future dispositional process. "There is in fact no fair way to offer a child the court's social services or the hope of such services and then turn around and use information gained during this period to determine coercive disposition."[9]

Even now, great care is taken to isolate the facts that could prove the allegations of a petition from the social information gathered during the intake investigation. But reflections of concern for the juvenile's rights are likely to be increasingly specific and formal.

DEFENSE ATTORNEYS

Bifurcation of juvenile court hearings is likely to increase the proportion of cases in which the minor and/or his parents are represented by an attorney. In the years since the *Gault* decision, in fact, there has been a distinct trend toward legal counsel in juvenile court hearings. And as the adversary nature of contested matters (see Chapter 8) continues to develop, the counsel's role as defense attorney will increase, at least during the jurisdictional phase. Participation of prosecutors in the jurisdictional phase of *contested* hearings in some states even further identifies legal counsel as a defense attorney.

Even in the dispositional phase, it seems likely that, in the future, there will be substantial disputes between the probation officers' recommendations to the court and the "dispositional desires" of the minor and/or his parents. Nonetheless, future juvenile court dispositions will relate to

[9]J. E. Glen, "Bifurcated Hearings in the Juvenile Court," *Crime and Delinquency*, Vol. 16, No. 3 (1970), 262.

services used by the juvenile court more than to the court itself. These services, as I have noted, tend to function more effectively when administered separately from the judicial function. But, in terms of the court itself, certain probabilities related to the jurisdictional hearing are noteworthy because of their relationship to the judicial function. A typical example of one such probability is the increasing concern with such criminal court concepts as *mens rea.*

MENS REA

Adult crime is considered to occur when an *actus reus* (illegal act) is committed with *mens rea* (illegal intent). The *parens patriae* principle in juvenile court hearing, of course, removed concern for intent to an analysis of causal and corrective factors. Even early juvenile courts generally considered *actus reus* as a symptom.

As future jurisdictional hearings in juvenile court place greater emphasis on adversary proof of allegations, a corresponding concern with *mens rea* (as defined in adult criminal courts) seems reasonable:

> Two different questions are often subsumed under the heading of *mens rea.* The first question is whether or not one's conduct was voluntary. The second is whether or not the person realized at the time that his conduct would, or might produce results of a certain kind—the element of foreseeability. In modern times, our attention has been focused upon one's realization of the consequences of his conduct. In early law, however, the emphasis was upon whether one's conduct was voluntary or involuntary. Both elements are required for criminal liability at common law, and difficulties and confusion arise only when they are not kept separate in one's thinking.[10]

Future concern with *mens rea* will likely be accompanied by a host of philosophical criminal court concepts: "Justice, though due to the accused, is due to the accuser also. The concept of fairness must not be strained till it is narrowed to a filament. We are to keep the balance true."[11] Concern for "balance" between offender and victim is as likely as concern for double jeopardy. These concepts have not been significant in juvenile court since the *Winship* decision established the standard for beyond-reasonable-doubt. But in the juvenile court of the future, increasing emphasis on such concepts is probable.

Again, at least the jurisdictional phase will become more formal. This trend has grown by leaps and bounds since the President's Commission pointed out in 1967 that there is "increasing evidence that . . . informal

[10]J. E. Westbrook, *"Mens Rea* in the Juvenile Court," *Journal of Family Law,* Vol. 5, No. 2 (1965), 125.

[11]Justice Benjamin N. Cardozo, *Snyder* v. *Massachusetts,* 291 U.S. 97, 122 (1934).

procedures, contrary to the original expectation, may themselves constitute a further obstacle to effective treatment of the delinquent to the
extent that they engender in the child a sense of injustice provoked by
seemingly all-powerful and challengeless exercise of authority by judges
and probation officers."[12] In a sense, future juvenile court procedures
will be a reversal of earlier procedures: "Formal criminal proceedings
were eliminated in favor of informal hearings. As if to emphasize the shift
from such concepts as criminal responsibility to that of protection and
guidance, nomenclature was changed."[13] The probability that the *parens
patriae* approach will be abandoned in the jurisdictional proceedings of
juvenile court derives from concern with rights and, hence, formal proceedings.

PROBATION SERVICES AND THE COURT

In terms of those probation functions related directly to the juvenile
court, the future court is likely to demonstrate increasing acceptance of
four recommendations offered in the Joint Commission's report.[14] First,
a probation officer "should have final responsibility for the management
of the court's intake processes, for the application of criteria governing
intake, for the method by which the intake staff channels cases into the
court process, and for the maintenance of liaison between intake staff and
various community agencies to which cases are diverted." Second, the
probation officer "should have control over the detention facility used by
the court though he need not manage it directly. The detention facilities
should be staffed and operated by a semi-autonomous unit subject to the
chief probation officer's supervision. This administrative device would
insure that all efforts of the detention staff would be effectively correlated
with those of the court's probation staff."

Third, the probation officer's "most important functions should be the
integration of services and coordination of the work of the various disciplines represented by members of the court staff. Interdisciplinary communication is essential. To perform this function, the chief probation
officer must have sufficient sophistication in the various helping skills to
coordinate the work of the probation counselor with that of the psychologist, the psychiatrist, or the physician." Fourth, "in addition to coordination of the various disciplines working in juvenile rehabilitation, the chief

[12]President's Commission on Law Enforcement and Administration of Justice, *The
Challenge of Crime in a Free Society* (Washington, D.C., 1967), p. 85.

[13]H. W. Sloane, "The Juvenile Court: An Uneasy Partnership of Law and Social Work,"
Journal of Family Law, Vol. 5, No. 2 (1965), 175.

[14]T. Rubin and J. T. Smith, *The Future of the Juvenile Court: Implications for Correctional Manpower and Training* (Washington, D.C.: Joint Commission for Correctional
Manpower Development, 1968), excerpts from pp. 58–59.

probation officer must keep himself informed about innovative work being done by the various disciplines in other courts and agencies."

A trend in this general direction is already developing in hundreds of jurisdictions throughout the nation—intake/detention coordination and program innovation, and recruiting, training, and administrative program continuity are increasingly removed from the judicial process.

PROGRAM MANAGEMENT SYSTEMS AND THE JUDICIARY:
DISTINCT DIFFERENCES

The relationship between the court and probation is of interest because it illustrates how the court works closely with a distinctly separate subsystem. Effective managerial and programming technology is sorely needed in both juvenile and criminal justice. But, for different reasons, this subsystem also should be independent of the court. For example, systems analysis may focus on probation more than juvenile court. "It might be that no optimal model of performance could be derived from the existing court system. Systems analysis would then call for examination of the subsystems which come closest to optimal performance. This would call for a study of what is desired from the court system and what could be achieved from available resources."[15]

The evolution of an effective managerial base for a complex operation appears to be a probation rather than a judicial problem. Among the reasons to believe this to be the case is the fact that "the courts are not a primary agency. All children need a family, a school, health care, social and recreational opportunities; but not all children need a juvenile court. Juvenile courts prevent delinquency by preventing recidivism. The prevention of initial delinquency is basically the job of the family and the primary agencies."[16] Of course, neither are police and probation officers now "primary agencies." But they are certainly the most primary agencies in the juvenile justice system and, as such, stand to profit most from improved management and systems analysis.

One conspicuous advantage to future managerial trends will be a probable reduction in such criticisms as the following:

> The necessity of processing large numbers of cases with diversified problems transforms juvenile courts into hierarchical organizations with divisions, departments, specialists, and routinized procedures. As such, they take on the qualities and problems of bureaucracy. Cases are passed from functionary to functionary and from one department to another, hence, decisions often are reached in piece-meal fashion or in consultations between various levels of authority. While there is a strain towards rationalized procedures, nevertheless

[15]Ibid., p. 63.
[16]Ibid., p. 67.

responsibility tends to be diffused, and conflicts between individual workers or between divisions are endemic. Group interaction within the court, routines, contingencies, and organizational requirements profoundly affect the fate of cases.

. . . Many of the difficulties of the juvenile court revolve around its character as an enterprise originally designed to use the power and authority of law to achieve ends not amenable to legal means. . . . If the problem domain of the juvenile court is to be made smaller and more specialized, other definitions of youth problems need to be developed and new means invented to deal with them. This can be accomplished by reorganizing existing agency resources or by inventing new types of organization, or both. In both instances, the organizational principle or objective will be that of bypassing the juvenile court process.[17]

Shifting managerial responsibilities away from the judicial should not only reduce criticism of the juvenile court but facilitate a frequently voiced recommendation:

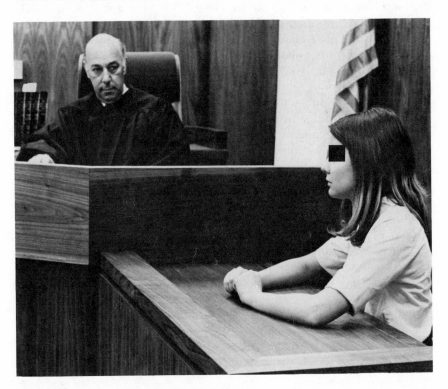

Photo by Charles Tado, County of Santa Clara, California

[17]E. M. Lemert, *Instead of Court: Diversion in Juvenile Justice* (Washington, D.C.: Public Health Service Publication, 1971), No. 2127, pp. 4–6, 18.

Changes in public policy aimed at narrowing the jurisdiction of the juvenile court and limiting the range of problems definable as delinquency can be formed by appellate rulings, legislation, and finding new ways of administering the law. In the past, appeals from juvenile court decisions have not been influential in constraining unwise action by juvenile court.[18]

PUBLIC OPINION

Notwithstanding the earlier suggestion that public concern can stimulate legislative response to problems that may ultimately involve the Supreme Court, the juvenile court (and all other segments of juvenile and criminal justice) is likely to experience greater *direct* impact from public opinion. While public opinion will remain capricious, even its temporary force effects substantial change. "Public concern with crime and delinquency is now at a height it has not reached in any recent historical period. . . . There are not only reputations but fortunes to be made by—or, at least, distributed to—criminologists whose research holds promise of developing better weapons for 'the war on crime.' "[19] While such concern forecasts a probable willingness to vote the taxes and bonds that underpin juvenile justice programming, this same concern also forecasts far less satisfaction with what many interpret as "legal double-talk" and "sociological hogwash" instead of results.

The day is coming when good intentions count for virtually nothing with a tax-paying public that continually finds itself criminally assaulted and its property stolen or maliciously destroyed. The juvenile court will doubtless feel the impact of this dissatisfaction just as directly as any other segment of juvenile or criminal justice.

Summary

This chapter dealt with the future of the juvenile court in the general context of reduced court load and increased services. Supreme Court influence was predicted to increase emphasis on bifurcated hearings and such formalities and legalities as defense attorneys and criminal court concepts.

The general increase in formality was cited as a basis for isolating juvenile court (particularly from probation) as a specific function of juvenile justice. The separation of probation and the judiciary was elaborated in terms of administrative variables and program management, which should increase as correctional programming improves through research.

[18]Ibid., p. 16.
[19]R. R. Korn, *Juvenile Delinquency* (New York: Thomas Y. Crowell Company, 1968), p. 4.

The influence of public opinion was considered in light of increasing public dissatisfaction with the juvenile justice system's lack of tangible remedies for delinquency.

Questions

1. Discuss Supreme Court involvement in future juvenile court procedures.
2. Relate legislative response to major social problems to the Supreme Court philosophy.
3. Explain the basis for predicting increased formality through bifurcated hearings.
4. Define *mens rea* and explain its implications for juvenile court.
5. Explain how you think the juvenile court should respond to a decrease in court cases.
6. Describe your impressions of the juvenile justice system on the basis of what you have read in this text. What changes do you think are necessary (not necessarily predictable) for: police, probation, court, corrections, and parole? Explain your answers.

Annotated References

ALLISON, J. E., "Counsel in the Juvenile Court," *Federal Probation,* Vol. 30, No. 1 (1966).

――――, "The Lawyer and His Juvenile Court Client," *Crime and Delinquency,* Vol. 12, No. 2 (1966).

CICOUREL, A. V., *The Social Organization of Juvenile Justice.* New York: John Wiley & Sons, Inc., 1968.

COFFEY, A. R., *Administration of Criminal Justice: A Management Systems Approach.* Englewood Cliffs, N.J.: Prentice-Hall, Inc., 1973. Elaboration of managerial techniques, including systems analysis, to generate administrative results.

GLEN, J. E., "Bifurcated Hearings in the Juvenile Court," *Crime and Delinquency,* Vol. 16, No. 3 (1970). Good background for this chapter's forecasted emphasis on bifurcated hearings.

KETCHAM, O. W., "The Unfulfilled Promise of the Juvenile Court," *Crime and Delinquency,* Vol. 97 (1961). Good background for entire chapter.

MENNEL, R. M., "Origins of the Juvenile Court: Changing Perspectives on the Legal Rights of Juvenile Delinquents," *Crime and Delinquency,* Vol. 18, No. 1 (1972). Elaboration of signs of greater formality in future juvenile court proceedings.

RUBIN, T., and J. T. SMITH, *The Future of Juvenile Court: Implications for Correctional Manpower and Training.* Washington, D.C., June, 1968. Outstanding review of most of the factors relevant to the juvenile courts of the future.

Author Index

Subject Index